Cycling Australia

S0-ARO-133

Cycling Australia

Bicycle Touring Throughout the Sunny Continent

Ian Duckworth

Covering the Australian Mainland and Tasmania

Bicycle Books – San Francisco

Copyright © Ian Duckworth, 1997

Printed in U.S.A.

Published by:
Bicycle Books, Inc.
1282 - 7th Ave
San Francisco, CA 94122

Distributed to the book trade by:

U.S.A.	National Book Network, Lanham, MD
Australia	Tower Books, Frenchs Forest, NSW
U.K.	Chris Lloyd Sales & Marketing Services, Poole, Dorset
Canada	Raincoast Book Distribution, Vancouver, BC

All photos by the author, except as credited

Maps by the author and Bicycle Books

Cover design by Kent Lytle, Lytle Design, Alameda,
based on a photograph of the Twelve Apolstles by the author

Frontispiece photo: riding through the forest on a dirt road in
Western Australia.

Publishers Cataloging-in-Publication Data
Duckworth, Ian, 1974–
Cycling Australia : Bicycle Touring Throughout the Sunny
Continent / Ian Duckworth. San Francisco: Bicycle Books, 1997.

224 p. : col. ill., maps; 21.6 cm.
Includes index

Summary: Gives background information and route descriptions
with route maps for 8 multi-day bicycle tours throughout the
Australian mainland and Tasmania.

ISBN 0-933201-76-1
LCCCN 96-84650

1. Bicycle touring - Autralia - Directories 2. Bicycle trails - Australia -
Directories 3. Australia - Bicycle touring - Directories
I. Authorship II. Title

Acknowledgments

I would like to thank all the people that helped me with the rather large task of putting this book together.

Special thanks go to my sometime riding companion Aziz El Bakush, whose death-defying antics on a fully laden touring bike still have me in awe.

I'm also deeply indebted to my father, who assisted with much of the research necessary for this publication and accompanied me on many of the rides.

Thanks also to my brother for doing a ride, as well as the rest of my family and friends for their support.

Finally, thanks go to the many wonderful people I've met on my cycling travels. It's good to know that there are so many adventurous souls out there, cycling the backroads somewhere, every day.

About the Author

Born and raised in Perth, Western Australia, Ian Duckworth is a law student at Murdoch University. He took to cycle touring while traveling around Europe during a year's break from his studies. With several thousand touring kilometers under his belt, he returned to Australia, and after a stint as a bicycle courier in the city, set about exploring his own

backyard by bike. The results of that exploration are detailed in the eight rides contained in this book.

This is his first publication, but he hopes to combine his interests in travel, writing, and photography many more times in the future. Away from the bike, he has also traveled extensively, backpacking in the U.S.A. and Europe, and visiting Asia several times.

Table of Contents

Part I. Background Information

Part II. The Routes

Chapter 1.
Why Cycle Touring in
Australia?

Cycling offers the perfect balance between really seeing and experiencing one place while having the ability to visit many different places. In the past I've done some hiking and walking, even spending some time on the Appalachian Trail, and while that was a tremendous experience, it is easy to get frustrated when the most ground you're likely to cover is 20 miles on a good day. At the other end of the scale I've also been on the typical whirlwind tour, spending a day or two in each capital city, attempting to see the whole of Europe in a couple of weeks, ending up really seeing little besides the inside of airport departure lounges. On a bike, however, you travel slowly enough so that you really take everything in. You notice what types of plants are growing at the roadside; you see people tending their gardens and animals grazing. You hear the birds, the insects, the howl of the wind, and the rumble of a farmer's tractor ploughing a field. You smell the

Along the Great Ocean Road—Cape Patton lookout near Apollo Bay.

flowers, freshly cut grass, and unfortunately sometimes even the remains of a road kill, but it all adds to the total experience, and at the end of the day you feel as if you know the place just about as well as anyone. At the same time, it is surprising just how much ground you can cover on a bike. On an average touring day you're likely to pedal fairly comfortably somewhere around 80 km (50 miles) over the course of a week adding up to a considerable 500 km (310 miles). At that rate, even in a country as large as Australia you can see a lot in a fairly limited time.

You're also unconstrained by timetables. You don't have to worry if the only bus from a small town leaves on a Wednesday or a Friday. When you're cycling you carry everything you need to be independent. You may ride into a place, like it and decide to stay a week, or on the other hand hate it and cycle on. The point is that unlike other forms of travel, you are free to choose when to stay and when to leave. If you're tired and have had enough, you can pull off the road and have a rest or even call it a day: you are master of your own destiny.

People, locals and fellow travelers alike, for some reason also seem almost universally to like cycle tourers. Some days I would almost get sick of waving back at motorists keen to wish me well. In villages and towns, people will come over and ask you about your trip, where you've come from and how far your going, often providing you with information on local beauty spots or even offering you a cold drink or a place to stay for the night. I think they appreciate the fact that you've taken the time to really explore and experience the land they're so proud of, instead of passing it by from the inside of an air-conditioned train traveling at 100 mph on its way between capital cities.

There is also a bond between fellow cycle tourers, unique among travelers. Every time I'd run across another cyclist, we would swap stories about places we'd been, hills we'd climbed and people we'd met, often exchanging tips and offering each other advice on good routes to take. Frequently we would end up cycling together for several days until our paths finally diverged, forming lasting friendships during the time spent together. Such a camaraderie is rare these days.

About This Guide

This book contains route descriptions for eight tours of differing lengths passing through all six Australian states. The rides have been specifically designed so that in most cases it is possible to start one tour where you finish another. By combining tours, you can ride a marathon tour from Adelaide to Brisbane and also complete a circumnavigation of Tasmania. The daily rides average about 80 km in length, a distance that you can cover fairly easily, with rides over 100 km rare and only appearing where unavoidable. Where possible, you cycle along quiet country roads through areas of natural, scenic beauty, avoiding highway travel where viable alternatives exist.

This book in no way pretends to be an exhaustive guide to good cycle tours in Australia. In such a big country there are countless opportunities for you to strike out and explore on your own, but as the rides in this book have already been thoroughly researched and ridden, you can be assured of some quality touring, with information on terrain, road conditions, weather, local attractions, and accommodation provided along the way.

Rides are presented in eight distinct tours, mainly linking capital cities. Descriptions of the rides are given day by day, with a summary of the tour at the start of each chapter, which includes a brief synopsis, distance, terrain, and touring time. Directions on how to get out of town and what roads to follow, as well as the distances to significant points such as towns and intersections, appear in the body of text along with a commentary on the scenery, local attractions, terrain, and road conditions. As an aid to navigation, and to get the most out of this book, I suggest you install a bike computer. By measuring the distance traveled each day, you can be aware of the proximity of an approaching turnoff or town. You'll also find that it offers many other worthwhile functions.

Maps

Although this book contains route maps of all the rides described, I suggest that you supplement these by purchasing maps of a suitable scale for the area in which you will be traveling. As Australia is so big, many maps are drawn to a very large scale, showing insufficient detail for the roads on which you'll be traveling. Look for a map with a scale of around 1:300 000 or less. Maps around this scale represent a good compromise between showing sufficient detail and having to buy a new sheet every couple of days. Look for them in book shops or gas stations.

Additional Information

Although I have endeavored to provide information on all the places featured in this book, in order to keep the book small enough to slip into your handlebar bag, I felt that it was both inappropriate and unnecessary to include too much extraneous detail. I therefore strongly recommend that you purchase a general travel guide such as Lonely Planet's *Outback Australia*.

Additional information can also be obtained through state tourist bureaus, as well as from specific cycling-oriented sections of state-based Departments of Transport, such as Bikewest in Western Australia.

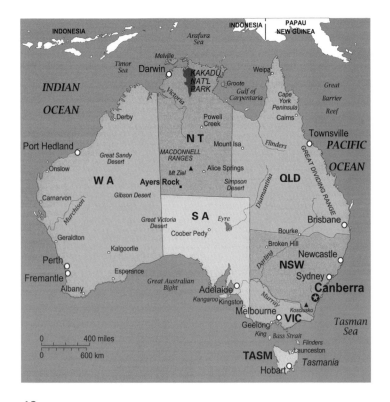

Chapter 2.
Australia: Country Information

Location and Geography

Australia is an island continent located in the southern hemisphere, with a land mass of some 7,682,300 sq. km, making it the world's sixth-largest country and approximately the same size as the contiguous United States. East to west it stretches approximately 4,000 km, and north to south it extends about 3,200 km, with a 36,735 km coastline, almost double that of the United States. Despite its enormous size, only 18 million people call Australia home, 86% of those in urban areas, making it one of the most sparsely populated countries on the globe.

Much of the interior of the country, commonly known as the outback, is arid and inhospitable, with approximately 30% of the country's total land mass being unsuitable for any agricultural use. Another 50% receives very little rain and can be used only for such activities as cattle farming, with each animal requiring an enormous area in which to graze. The remaining 20% supports a range of agricultural and pastoral industries and is concentrated in the east, southeast, and southwest of the country, roughly reflecting the geographical distribution of the population.

The country is divided into six states and two territories comprising New South Wales (NSW), Victoria (Vic), Queensland (Qld), Western Australia (WA), South Australia (SA), and the island state of Tasmania (Tas). The two territories are the Northern Territory (NT) and the Australian Capital Territory (ACT) where Canberra, the nation's capital and seat of government, is located. The bulk of the population inhabits a narrow coastal strip of land extending along the east coast. Sydney is the biggest of the Australian cities, followed by Melbourne, Brisbane, Perth, and Adelaide.

Geologically, Australia is the oldest of the continents, with estimates dating its landmass to be more than 1 billion years old. A narrow, fertile strip of land extends along the east coast of the country, hemmed in by the Pacific Ocean and the Great Dividing Range, the eroded remnants of a once-mighty mountain range that is now high enough to attract reliable winter snowfall in the alpine regions near the NSW/Victorian border. Mt. Kosciusko is the highest peak at 2,228 m (7,310 ft.) high. To the west of the range, the country gets increasingly dry and harsh and is predominantly flat, apart from such features as the MacDonnell ranges and Ayres Rock near Alice Springs. Another small mountain range stretches down the southern part of the west coast, to the east of which is a fertile coastal area bordered by the Indian Ocean. The north and interior of West Australia (the biggest state) are vast and largely inhospitable, but contain areas of vast mineral riches with enormous deposits of iron ore, gold, diamonds, and natural gas. The far north or top end of the country is tropical, with high rainfall over the summer months or wet season, but practically none at other times of the year.

History

The first Australians, the Aboriginal people, have inhabited the continent for at least 40,000 years. They are thought to have migrated from somewhere in southern Asia, but exactly where is not known. Traditionally they were semi-nomadic hunter-gatherers, roaming in small extended-family groups over a defined tribal area or "country," in search of food. During their travels they also carried out necessary sacred and religious ceremonies and rituals often associated with ensuring that the land would continue to provide and that sacred beings were accorded due recognition.

Society was organized within an intricate kinship and religious system where behavior and responsibilities were subject to strict rules and observances. Traditional Aboriginal people had a rich oral literature system of song cycles and art, which expressed their complex systems of belief. At the time of the arrival of Captain Arthur Phillips' first fleet in 1788, there were roughly 300,000 Aboriginal people living in Australia in several hundred tribal and linguistic groupings.

Prior to white settlement of Australia, several European sailors and navigators had passed by and even landed on Australian shores. Luis Vaez de Torres, a Spanish navigator, passed through the strait between Australia and Papua New Guinea that now bears his name. Dutch sailors Dirk Hartog, Abel Tasman, and William de Vlamingh charted various parts of the west and south coasts, and in 1770 Captain James Cook sighted the east coast of Australia and later claimed it in the name of Britain.

European occupation of Australia began in earnest when the "First Fleet" arrived at Port Jackson (now Sydney) in 1788 with 1,400 people, including 736 convicts. The British government, which had previously shipped its convicts to America until that country won its independence, now began the mass transportation of felons to Australia. The transportation of convicts lasted until 1850 on the east coast and Tasmania. In the Swan River Colony (now Western Australia), it did not begin until 1850 and ceased in 1868. It was a brutal period of harshness and great cruelty for many of the convicts, but it is doubtful that Europeans would have settled successfully in this harsh country without convict labor.

The effect of white occupation/invasion was disastrous for the Aboriginal people, some of whom were exterminated by force and many of whom died from introduced diseases such as measles, smallpox, and syphilis. The acquisitive and hierarchical culture of the invading British had nothing in common with the egalitarian and spiritual culture of the Aborigines, who soon became outsiders in their own land.

Throughout the 19th century, Europeans, mainly British, continued to settle Australia. In 1850 the British government passed the Australian Colonies Act, which empowered the colonies to set up legislatures and draw up constitutions. Victoria set up the first legislature in 1851, and New South Wales drew up the constitution in 1855. In 1891, a draft federation was drawn up, and in 1901 a federation of six states, the former colonies, was set up with an Australian federal constitution. Australia was now a self-governing nation.

During the 20th century, Australia continued to grow in population and prosperity, developing an economy that until the 1950s was heavily dependent on rural industries such as wool and wheat. The 1960s saw the mineral boom, particularly in Western Australia and Queensland, with coal, iron ore, and bauxite becoming huge export earners. The primary sector of the economy, raw materials and agriculture, is still the major contributor to Australia's export dollar, but in recent years the economy has started to become more sophisticated and diversified.

After World War II, Australia's mainly Anglo-Saxon population began to diversify, and a huge migration program began, which included tens of thousands of displaced persons from war-torn Europe. Non-British migration from all over Europe increased in the 1950s and 1960s. By the 1970s the last vestiges of the old "white Australia" policy had finally been abandoned, and since that time there has been large-scale migration from southeast Asia, the Indian subcontinent, the Middle East, and parts of Africa, as well as Latin America and the South Pacific. Australia is now one of the most multicultural countries in the world, with more than 25% of the population born overseas and a further 25% having at least one parent born overseas.

Successive governments have managed this diversity very positively, with the result that there is very little community disharmony due to ethnic or racial issues. There is still much to be done, however, to raise the living standard of the Aboriginal people, who remain by far the most disadvantaged sector of the population.

Three themes dominate much of the discussion about Australia's future. First, many now believe that Australia's destiny lies much more with the Asia-Pacific region than with Britain and Europe—certainly this is true in relation to the economy. Second, there is a desire to achieve reconciliation with the Aboriginal people over their mistreatment in the past. The third theme of the nineties is republicanism, with a recent poll showing that a majority wants the country to release the queen of England of her duties down under.

Weather and Climate

Being such a large country, Australia experiences significant variations in weather around the land at any one time, with climatic conditions ranging from temperate in the far south to tropical in the far north. With Australia situated squarely in the southern hemisphere, the seasons are the reverse of those in the northern hemisphere; the summer extends from December to February and winter from June through August. Summers in the south are generally hot and dry, winters mild and wet. Seasonal variations become less noticeable the further north you travel; there are basically only two seasons, the dry (winter) and the wet (summer) in the top end. Extreme summer temperatures of over 40° C are not uncommon, particularly in WA, SA, and inland areas.

Chapter 3.
Getting to Australia

A total of 48 international airlines operate direct to and from Australia, though not all of them serve all Australian state capitals. Some of the major carriers operating from various destinations are listed below. This is not an exhaustive list, as there are still other airlines that may couple with those listed below in differing combinations of connecting flights. In these days of cut-throat competition in the travel industry, travel agencies and flight centers have assembled a bewildering array of mix-and-match packages. Often special deals on domestic flights within Australia are available, as well as discounts on accommodation and bus fares, or there may be a free trip thrown in. A round-the-world fare may sometimes be as cheap as, or cheaper than, a regular fare—and the cost of the ticket will usually include a flight between two Australian cities, such as Sydney–Perth or Sydney–Darwin.

Airlines may differ in relation to their bicycle policy. Most ask that bikes are securely boxed. Many simply count the bike as part of your luggage weight allowance; however, some airlines may charge a small surcharge. Make sure that you clarify each airline's policy while you are shopping around.

A chance encounter with English touring cyclists near the Coorong, South Australia.

From:	Airline
U.S.A.	Qantas, United, American Airlines, Air New Zealand, Canadian Airlines, Continental
Canada	Qantas, Canadian Airlines
U.K.	Qantas, British Airways, Singapore Airlines, Malaysian Air Services
New Zealand	Polynesian Airlines, Air New Zealand, Qantas, Singapore Airlines, Thai Airways, United, Aerolineas Argentinas, Malaysian Air Services
South Africa	Qantas, South African Airways

Passport and Visa Requirements

Everyone traveling to Australia requires a valid passport and a visa. With the exception of New Zealand citizens, who simply fill out an in-flight card en route to Australia, all other travelers must obtain a visa prior to arrival.

You can apply for a visa at any Australian embassy, consulate, or high commission. To obtain a visa you must be able to demonstrate that you have the funds to support yourself during your stay and that you have an air ticket out of Australia. Alternatively you may be granted a visa if you have a sponsor who undertakes to accommodate and maintain you during your visit. Your sponsor may be required to supply a statement of income to support his or her sponsorship.

Visas are valid for either three or six months, and it is advisable to apply for your visa at least one month prior to your flight to Australia. Under certain circumstances visas may be renewed, providing there are compelling reasons. For information about visa renewal you should contact the nearest branch of the Department of Immigration and Ethnic Affairs—there are branches in Canberra and all Australian state capitals.

Customs and Immigration Procedures

Shortly before arriving in Australia, the aircraft cabin crew will give you a *Traveller's Statement* to fill out. You will also be asked to complete an *Incoming Passenger Card*. On arrival you will first proceed to immigration, where you will be required to show your passport and other travel documents. You can then go to the baggage hall to collect your baggage. Next you proceed to customs where you will be asked to follow either the "green channel" if you have nothing to declare, or the "red channel" if you have something to declare. Customs officers may search your luggage in either channel.

As with most countries, there are severe penalties for failing to declare dutiable articles. There are also very severe penalties for being found in possession of prohibited substances (drugs) and a variety of other obviously dangerous or undesirable items. If you are in any doubt about what you are allowed to take into Australia, check with the Australian authorities at the time of your visa application.

Personal effects are admitted into Australia free of duty, provided that they are your own property, are for your own use, and are not intended for sale or any other commercial purposes. In addition, there are certain duty-free concessions, as follows:

Alcohol

1 liter of alcoholic liquor, including wine beer or spirits, per person over 18 years of age

Tobacco

250 grams of tobacco products (250 cigarettes are deemed the equivalent of 250 grams for customs purposes)

Other goods

Other goods obtained overseas, provided they are i nted or received as gifts, are free of duty and sales tax in Australia up to a value of A$400 per person over 18 or A$200 per person under 18.

Currency

There is no limit to the amount of Australian and/or foreign cash that may be brought into Australia, but amounts of A$5,000 or more, or the equivalent in other currencies, have to be declared on entry. (This provision applies to cash and not to traveler's cheques or other monetary instruments.)

Quarantine

Australia has strict quarantine regulations, which so far have served the country well, as it is free from many of the human, plant, and animal diseases that are present in other parts of the world. You must declare all foodstuffs, goods made from animal products, plants and plant products, including wooden articles. Sometimes you will be asked if you have recently spent time on a farm—and they may want to look at your shoes in case there are traces of mud or soil.

Vaccination

Australia has only one compulsory vaccination applicable to some visitors. People arriving in Australia within six days of leaving a yellow fever–infected area must have a valid yellow fever vaccination certificate. A clear ten days must have elapsed between vaccination and arrival. This applies also to travelers coming to Australia through countries considered to be yellow fever–infected areas.

Any traveler in the above category arriving without a valid vaccination certificate will be isolated for the remainder of the six-day incubation period.

Departure Tax

When leaving Australia, a departure tax of A$27 is levied on all people age 12 years and over. You can pay the departure tax either at the airport or at any post office.

Chapter 4.
Australia:
An Orientation

This chapter provides the information you need to familiarize yourself with day-to-day happenings in Australian society, ensuring that you'll know what to expect. Included is practical information on such things as accommodation, food and drink, safety hints, weights and measures, and opening hours. There's even a quick guide to Australian English, so you won't be baffled if someone says "G'day, I'm crook mate. Where's the dunny?"

Types of Accommodation:

The choice of accommodation in cities is as you would expect, both wide and prolific, ranging from youth hostels to five-star resorts. In the majority of sizeable country towns, however, you'll likely encounter three main forms of accommodation: motels, pubs, and caravan parks. Thankfully there are also an increasing number of youth hostels and backpacker establishments opening across the country.

The Canberra YHA is a typical modern purpose-built hostel.

Motels:

Price Range: from $35 double.
Motels generally offer a room with one or two double beds, a bathroom, color TV, air conditioner, facilities for making tea and coffee, and a fridge. Most motels display a star rating on the sign outside, usually awarded by the motor vehicle association for that state (e.g., NRMA, RACV), giving you a good idea of the comfort level you can expect. Two stars represent a basic but clean room, whereas you might find a swimming pool, restaurant, better decor, and bigger rooms in a three- or four-star complex. Needless to say, price generally increases with the number of stars, with the bulk of motels you're likely to encounter being in the two- and three-star category. Motels can be quite a good value for two people, offering privacy and comfort after a long day in the saddle. If you are traveling alone, however, the price may be less attractive, as the single room tariff generally isn't much less than the double rate, maybe $5 or $10.

Pubs and Hotels:

Price Range: from $15 single, $25 double.
Country pubs seem to be pretty similar in towns all over Australia. Often housed in grand old buildings, they usually offer basic accommodation in a sparsely furnished room, often containing just an old bed, a wardrobe, and a bare light bulb. Although not five-star luxury, pubs are usually a good value, with the added bonus of meals and drinks available just downstairs. It may be a good idea to ask before you check in whether there are any bands playing that night, as it's been my experience that the floor of your room isn't a particularly effective insulator against noise. Also bear in mind that weekends are likely to be noisier. A pair of ear plugs is likely to prove a worthwhile investment.

Caravan (Mobile Home) Parks:

Price Range: from $8 per site.
Caravan parks offer tent sites and often accommodation in on-site vans or small cabins. All have shower and toilet facilities, while some may offer cooking areas, laundries, and even swimming pools. They tend to vary considerably in quality, and outside of popular holiday areas you'll likely have to search for a place to pitch your tent between permanently anchored caravans. I must admit that, as a

solo traveler, I am not a big fan of caravan parks, as they charge a flat rate for tent sites regardless of the number of people or the size of your tent. It's a bit irritating having to pay the same amount to erect my tiny one-man tent as a family of eight next doors pays for a tent of circus-like proportions. Often you get little more than a hot shower for your money. Cabins and vans can often be a good option if you are traveling in a larger group.

Youth Hostels and Backpacker Hostels:

Price Range: from $8, average price $12–$14.
These establishments are a real asset to the budget traveler and cyclist. They offer budget accommodation in single-sex dormitory-style rooms usually containing 4–8 beds, with limited numbers of double and single rooms generally available. Most have kitchens and common areas as well as shared bathroom facilities. Some also offer various recreational facilities and organized tours. They can vary considerably in quality, although most are of a good standard.

There are two main types of hostels, those associated with the YHA (Youth Hostels Association)—a worldwide non-profit organization of over 5,300 hostels (more than 130 of them in Australia)—and independent backpacker establishments. Usually, you must be a member to stay at YHA hostels—if you are not, you may not be allowed to stay or you may be charged a higher rate. If you are going to be traveling for any length of time, membership is well worthwhile and is available from YHA offices in all capital cities and most hostels. Despite the name, membership is open to people of all ages. YHA hostels don't allow the use of sleeping bags and insist that you have a sleep-sheet (sheet and pillow-slip in one). These can be rented, but it makes better sense to purchase one from an outdoor store or the hostel itself.

Backpacker establishments, or simply "backpacker's," are often family-run businesses and, like YHA hostels, offer clean, cheap accommodation. You don't need to be a member, although because of the lack of regulation, quality can vary more than is generally the case with YHA hostels. Having said this, there are many excellent backpacker hostels often offering facilities that are superior to their YHA counterparts.

Hostels are most commonly found in cities and popular holiday regions, although thankfully they are increasingly spreading to country areas as well. Throughout the book, I have mentioned these hostels where they exist along the route.

National Parks and State Parks:

Camping areas are often available in national parks. Some offer basic facilities, while in others it's a case of getting back to nature. Bear in mind that fees may be levied in some parks. As always with camping, be aware of restrictions concerning campfires, and be sure to carry all your rubbish out with you.

Free Camping:

Although I don't really recommend free camping, sometimes you may find yourself with no option. Be discreet about it and try to ensure you're not visible from the road. Respect private property (ask permission if necessary), be careful with fire, and clean up when you leave.

Food and Drink

Food in Australia is cheap, varied, and plentiful, and there is some wonderful local produce. The range of climates from tropical to Mediterranean to cool/temperate means that there is a huge variety of fruit and vegetables always in season. Australian-grown fruit available at different times includes mangoes, melons, paw paws, bananas, citrus, stone fruits, apples, pears, and berries, the latter from the cooler climes of Tasmania and Victoria. The cultural diversity of the population also means that you can obtain all your favorite varieties of cheese, sausage, and ethnic specialties, and there is an abundance of seafood and high-quality meat. Most state capitals have excellent fresh food markets, which are fun to shop in. The vast Queen Victoria Market in Melbourne is particularly good.

Drinks

Australia has the reputation of being a nation of zealous beer drinkers. Certainly the "amber fluid," as it is known, is still very popular and consumed in large quantities in some quarters. The good news, however, is that Australia has a wonderful wine industry. Oz wine, once derided as second-rate, has built an impressive reputation around the world for quality, taste, and sheer class. You can buy some very tasty stuff from around $6–7, or you can pay several hundred dollars for a twenty-year-old Penfolds Grange Hermitage, one of the world's great reds—or you can spend anything in between. Major wine-growing areas include the Hunter Valley in New South Wales, the Barossa Valley in South Australia, and the Swan Valley and Margaret River areas in Western Australia.

The last few years have seen a burgeoning of bistros and trendy street cafes, which means that the standard of coffee is now pretty good. It generally has a good robust flavor, particularly in the many ethnic Italian cafes and restaurants. Tea is still very popular, especially in the country.

Eating Out

Australia's culturally diverse population means that in the major cities you can find just about any kind of cuisine that you like; it's just a matter of deciding how much you want to pay.

At the budget end of the scale, Asian-style food halls, a feature of most major cities, are good value. For $4–8, depending on the size of the serving, you can choose from cuisines such as Cantonese, Indian, Malaysian, Vietnamese, Korean, Italian, Lebanese, vegetarian, or roasts. You will also find all the major pizza and hamburger fast-food chains and the ubiquitous fish and chip shops, where you can eat your fill for about $4. Counter meals in pubs are also worth considering. You can often buy a substantial main course such as a roast, a steak, or pasta for roughly $8–14.

When you eat in a restaurant, check to see if it is BYO. This means "bring your own" wine or beer. Most restaurants these days are licensed, which means that they generally sell you wine at a substantial mark-up on the retail price of the wine. A BYO restaurant enables you to save money by buying your own wine before you arrive at the restaurant. Mostly you don't get charged corkage; and if you do, it is no more than a dollar per head.

In country towns the choice of restaurant is more restricted, and food preferences tend toward the more traditional Anglo-Saxon fare—roasts, steaks, and fish and chips can be found on the menus of most country cafes and pubs. Another country town institution (though they can be found in cities as well) is the RSL club. RSL stands for "Returned Services League," an ex-servicemen's (veterans) organization. Someone will readily sign you in at the club, where you can obtain meals at reasonable prices and have a drink at the bar if you wish.

Australian eating habits have changed considerably over the last twenty years, with strong influences from Southeast Asia and the Mediterranean. At the fine-dining end of the scale, a distinctive Australian cuisine is emerging that fuses these influences and takes full advantage of the huge array of top-quality local produce.

Does Australia have a national dish? Well, sort of. The closest thing would have to be the Aussie meat pie, served hot, smothered in tomato ketchup, and frequently consumed at the "footy" (football game). It is calorie laden and not highly nutritious, but it is tasty and cheap at under $2. You should try at least one while you are in Australia. Vegemite, a sandwich spread made from yeast extract, and often eaten on toast for breakfast, is another distinctive Australian offering that you should try at least once.

Health and Safety Precautions

In most respects, Australia is a safe and friendly country for overseas visitors. It is a stable democracy with no civil strife or the kind of urban gang problems that are found in some countries. It has a first-class health and hospital system whose practitioners operate at a very high standard. As of the 1991 census, there were 230 doctors per 100,000 of population. With the exception of HIV/AIDS, which has remained at a very low level of prevalence, there are none of the serious epidemic diseases that are endemic in many countries.

Australian citizens are covered by a universal health care system called Medicare, which provides free basic hospital and medical coverage in return for a 1.4% levy on income. There is also a private health system that many Australians choose to belong to, with health insurance companies offering a variety of packages to fully or partially cover costs.

As a visitor, you will not be covered by Medicare, unless you are a citizen of one of the following countries with which Australia has a reciprocal health care agreement. These countries are Finland, the Netherlands, Sweden, the U.K., and New Zealand. A reciprocal health care agreement for a six-month period is also in place for citizens of Italy and Malta.

If you are a citizen of any country other than those covered by an agreement, I strongly recommend that you take out some form of health insurance prior to arriving in Australia—most general travel insurance offers differing levels of health coverage. If you are from one of the countries covered by an agreement, you may still wish to check out the details to make sure you are aware of, and happy with, the coverage. Finally, if you do arrive in Australia without health insurance and then decide you want coverage, there are companies that will provide it. You should ask a major travel agent or the Department for Immigration and Ethnic Affairs for details.

Notwithstanding the generally high standard of health and medical facilities, there are a number of areas where you need to take sensible precautions. No doubt you will have heard lurid and exotic tales of people in Australia taken by crocodiles and sharks, or bitten by deadly snakes on land and in the sea. There have certainly been some celebrated cases, but they are very rare. Nevertheless, if you are in places where there are sharks, crocodiles, and venomous snakes, take sensible precautions, such as not swimming in water that crocodiles are known to frequent (in all cases, in the far north of the country). Snakes usually make every effort to avoid humans, and if you are by remote chance unlucky enough to get bitten, try to identify the snake and seek medical advice as soon as possible.

Most urban beaches are patrolled by life guards, called "surf life savers," and safe swimming areas are usually clearly marked by red and yellow flags. If you are going to swim on very remote beaches, it is a good idea to seek some reputable advice on safety matters, from rips and currents to the prevalence of any dangerous marine animals. In general, the beaches in the north of the country—northern Queensland, the Northern Territory, and the northern parts of Western Australia, are the most dangerous in terms of highly venomous creatures such as box jellyfish, stonefish, and some varieties of sea snakes. Sharks are found all round the coast, but shark attacks remain a rarity.

Personal Security and Road Safety

Australian cities are pretty safe places generally, but you do need to exercise a little common sense. There may be one or two areas that are a bit risky to venture into at night, and you would need to be guided by local knowledge on this particular question. Bicycle theft does occur, so always secure your bike with one or more good locks, and preferably don't let it out of your sight for too long.

In the route descriptions in this book, you will be forewarned if some of the sections of the road pose any undue hazards. Some stretches of the main inter-city routes are used by large numbers of big trucks. If you are traveling on one of these roads, you will need to be especially careful. However, the tours in this book have been designed as much as possible to avoid very busy roads, and traffic on most Australian country roads is quite light.

For the most part you simply need to exercise a little common sense and discretion to avoid risks to your personal safety—for example, rather than cycle through the busy outer suburbs to reach the center of a city, why not travel with your bike on the train? In most cases it is possible. A little bit of lateral thinking in the odd difficult situation will ensure that you have a safe and enjoyable stay in Australia.

Australian English

Australia's national language is English, although you will undoubtedly hear other languages spoken, given the ethnic diversity of the population. If you travel to the Pilbara and Kimberley regions of Western Australia, the "top end" of the Northern Territory, central Australia, and northern Queensland, you may also hear various Aboriginal languages spoken.

Australian English is spoken with a distinctive "Aussie" accent and is rich in idioms and colorful expressions, some of which may baffle you at first. The table on the next page contains a few examples of the local lingo in no particular order.

You won't be too baffled by what you hear, and you may even find yourself wanting to collect some of the more colorful expressions. If this kind of thing interests you, you can buy publications that list all known Aussie expressions.

Australian	plain English
G'day	hello
rego	car registration
how ya goin	how are you
garbo	garbage man
beaut	excellent
smoko	short work break
full	drunk
truckie	truck driver
pissed	drunk
bikie	cyclist
pom	English person
barbie	barbecue
Kiwi	New Zealander
sheila	woman
wup wup	isolated area
wharfie	waterside worker
brekkie	breakfast
crook	ill, not well
tea	evening meal
dunny	toilet (U.S. bathroom, restroom)
you've got buckleys	no chance
arvo	afternoon
your shout	your round (drinks)
dill	foolish person
larrikin	mischievous person
hoon	wild person, tear-away
chook	chicken

Mail Services

Australia Post is Australia's national postal service, though there are also many courier and transport services serving the business community.

The cost of sending a letter anywhere in Australia is currently 45c, with next-day delivery to state capitals. There is a range of options for mailing items overseas, depending on how fast you want them to get there. For top-priority delivery, International Express Post will deliver within 2–4 days to major business centers in 180 countries. This service applies to everything from letters to parcels up to 20 kg. All items are bar coded for track trace of mail and include an automatic $100 insurance. Additional insurance is available at extra cost.

Air Mail gives you delivery within 7 days to over 200 countries. For some cities, delivery is in the 3–5 day range. As with Express Post, Air Mail is suitable for everything from a letter to a 20 kg parcel. Economy Air Mail is cheaper and slower than Air Mail, offering delivery within 7–14 days. The cheapest way to mail home is Sea Mail, which is ideal for heavier items when speed is not critical.

For travelers who have not decided where exactly they will be staying at any given destination, the "Poste Restante" facility is useful. Simply mark the item "Poste Restante" and address it to the post office in the city you will be traveling to. When you reach that destination, you will be able to pick up the article on production of your passport.

Telephone Services

The major telephone companies in Australia are Telstra and Optus. Local calls from public telephones are 40c and are not time-limited. Public phones can be found in booths outside post offices and in the street, or in some shops and delis. Long-distance calls, known as STD (Subscriber Trunk Dialling) within Australia and ISD (International Subscriber Dialling) to overseas destinations, are charged by the minute. The rate depends on what time of day or of the week the call is made. Both Telstra and Optus offer a range of special deals. Calls early in the morning and in the evening are generally cheaper, and there are some big discounts at weekends. Special offers keep changing, so it's best to give Telstra and Optus a call. You can call STD or ISD from most public phones, but you will need to find out the right codes for your country of destination. You can get the codes and information on how to dial STD and ISD from the phone book.

Public phones may be either coin or card operated. Phone cards can be purchased from post offices, newsagents, and some delis for $5, $10, $20, and $50.

Opening Times

In recent years, the opening hours of Australian retail shops and businesses have become increasingly deregulated. However, don't expect what happens in the major cities to necessarily occur in the country. In major cities, shops are open at least six days per week (Monday through Saturday) and in some cases seven days. Opening hours of most shops are 9:00 AM–5:30 PM. There is also late-night-shopping on at least one night per week in most major cities, usually on a Thursday or Friday. In smaller towns, shops generally close at midday on Saturday and don't reopen until Monday.

If you need something outside normal shopping hours, delis (delicatessens) stay open until late at night and sell basic grocery items. In the cities there are also 24-hour stores, late-night pharmacies, and petrol stations that sell groceries.

Liquor stores stay open during the evening, with hours differing from state to state. Pubs usually open at 10:00 A.M. or 11:00 A.M. and close any time from 11:00 P.M. onwards, though hours are shorter on Sundays and vary between states.

Banking hours vary a little but are usually 9:30 A.M.– 4:00 P.M. Monday to Thursday and 9:30 A.M.–5:00 P.M. on Friday. In the cities and larger country towns you will find plenty of ATMs (automatic teller machines), but in smaller country towns there may be no ATMs.

Post offices are open from 9:00 A.M.–5:00 P.M. Monday to Friday, with some now opening on Saturday mornings.

Office hours of most businesses and government departments are 8:30 A.M.–5:00 P.M. withslight variations.

Finally, there are several public holidays when banks and most shops and businesses are closed. Some apply to the nation as a whole, others are peculiar to particular states. The major national public holidays are as follows:

New Year's Day	January 1 (following Monday if on weekend)
Australia Day	January 26
Good Friday	
Easter Monday	
Anzac Day	April 25
Queen's Birthday	June 12 (1st Monday in October in WA)
Christmas Day	December 25
Boxing Day	December 26

Weights and Measures

Australia uses the metric system of weights and measures. If you're unfamiliar with the metric system, here are some equivalents to help you figure it out.

Mass		
1 gram (g)	=	0.0353 ounces
1 kilogram (kg)	=	2.20 pounds
Volume		
1 liter (l)	=	1.76 pints
Temperature		
1°C (Celsius)	=	32°F (Fahrenheit)
37.2°C	=	100°F
Length		
1 centimeter (cm)	=	0.394 inches
1 meter (m)	=	3.28 feet/1.09 yards
1 kilometer (km)	=	0.621 miles
Area		
1 square meter	=	10.8 square feet
1 square km	=	0.386 square miles
1 hectare	=	2.47 acres

Currency

Australia uses the decimal system of currency, with the basic monetary units being dollars ($) and cents (c). Coins are available in the following denominations: 5c, 10c, 20c, 50c, $1, and $2; notes come in: $5, $10, $20, $50, and $100 values.

Although foreign exchange rates can fluctuate considerably, here are a few exchange rates valid at the time of writing to help you plan your trip.

U.S.	$1	=	$1.33 AUD
U.K.	£1	=	$2.08 AUD
Canada	$1	=	$1.00 AUD
South Africa	1R	=	$0.36 AUD
New Zealand	$1	=	$0.88 AUD

Chapter 5.
Touring in Australia: Practical Considerations

The Best Times to Cycle

No matter what time of year you arrive in Australia, there's always somewhere offering suitable weather conditions. In general, for cycling in the southern states, which are the focus of this book, autumn (March–May) and spring (September–November) probably offer the best conditions, with mild to cool temperatures and moderate rainfall in most areas. Summers can be very dry and very hot especially in WA and SA, but may offer good conditions in Victoria and Tasmania, where temperatures tend to be milder. Conversely, Victoria, alpine areas, and Tasmania get quite cold in winter, with milder conditions in other states. If heading into the far north, winter or the dry season (July and August) are probably the best months, as it can get unbearably hot, humid, and wet in summer.

Dealing with the Heat

Australia has the highest rate of skin cancer in the world, and after a while under our summer sun you'll know why. Its rays can be intense, and if you arrive from the northern hemisphere when it is winter back home and summer in Australia, burning can occur in next to no time. Spending long hours each day in the saddle makes you particularly vulnerable to sun damage. Even if the weather isn't all that hot, you can still get burnt. In order to avoid spending your vacation immobilized by painful sunburn, take the following precautions.

1. Always apply an spf 15+ sunscreen to exposed areas of skin, and reapply frequently throughout the day, particularly if you are sweating a lot.

2. Wear a hat under your helmet. It looks kind of silly but is preferable to getting burnt.

3. Wear a light-colored, long-sleeved shirt, preferably with a high collar to protect the back of your neck, which is a particularly vulnerable area.

4. Wear gloves to protect the backs of your hands.

5. In hot weather, try to get up early and cycle in the cool of the morning. Have a siesta and rest in the shade in the heat of the day. Resume cycling in the late afternoon.

Water Precautions

Warning

Australia is a large, sparsely populated country, often with considerable distances between population centers, particularly if you are "off the beaten track." In the summer months in many areas, the temperature can be very hot—in the tropical north, it may be very hot most of the year. If you are cycling under these conditions, it is therefore essential to take plenty of water with you and check on the availability of fresh water along the way before setting off.

It is not advisable to cycle through isolated outback or desert regions where there may be no obtainable source of fresh water or habitation for hundreds of miles. If you do consider undertaking such trips, even with considerable backup support, it is essential to inform the local police (who will almost certainly urge you not to go).

Staying Hydrated

Extreme heat coupled with exertion makes it very easy to become dehydrated while cycling under the Australian sun. You can become seriously dehydrated without even knowing it: it is imperative that you drink regularly. In many cases, there are no places to get water between towns; it is essential to fill all of your water containers before setting off on each leg of your trip. It's also a good idea to drink your fill before leaving town. You should allow at least 500 ml of water per hour of cycling in warm conditions; so, ideally, you should have the ability to carry at least 5 or 6 liters. This is easily done with two large water bottles and a 4-liter water bag.

Although many Australian streams and creeks contain pure, fresh water, there are plenty that do not and may be fouled by livestock, algae, bacteria, or other contaminants. If you are unsure about a water source's purity, purify it before drinking by boiling, filtration, or chemical treatment.

One final tip. If staying in a youth hostel or somewhere else with a freezer, it's a good idea to stick your water bottle in the fridge overnight (remember to get it in the morning). The frozen bottle should keep your water icy cool for quite a while, making a refreshing change from the lukewarm liquid that you will otherwise have to endure.

Road and Traffic Rules

All cyclists who are unfamiliar with Australian road conditions and traffic rules should start by digesting at least the following essential information:

☐ In Australia you ride/drive on the left-hand side of the road.

☐ Distances are measured in km.

☐ Wearing seat belts in motor vehicles is compulsory.

☐ Cycle helmets are compulsory.

☐ In almost all states, the maximum legal blood alcohol is .05%.

☐ At unmarked intersections, you give way to the vehicle on your right.

☐ On dual-use cycle paths (paths for use by cyclists and pedestrians), cyclists give way to pedestrians.

☐ Cyclists are not permitted on freeways.

☐ With one or two small differences, Australian road signs follow international standards in graphics and design.

☐ Some back roads in country areas are unsealed (dirt) roads, and can be in poor condition especially after wet weather.

If you intend to drive a motor vehicle during your stay, you will need to obtain a more detailed knowledge of the traffic code. Every state police department or Road Traffic Authority publishes a comprehensive booklet detailing road traffic rules and required driving standards.

The RAC (Royal Automobile Club), and the NRMA (in NSW), are major motoring organizations that provide all sorts of touring information and are a good source of reasonably priced road maps.

Generally, Australian roads are maintained in good condition; however, take extra care on unsealed roads. As mentioned, their condition may vary due to weather conditions or whether or not they have been recently graded. Bear in mind if you are riding on unsealed roads that they can be slippery and hazardous, particularly if you are traveling downhill, so it is best to slow down on those stretches. Also, if your route does include some dirt sections, remember to allow yourself more time than if you are traveling on a sealed road.

In all parts of Australia there are sometimes long stretches of road between population centers, with few or perhaps no places to obtain food and drink. The route descriptions in this book will forewarn you when this is the case, but if you are striking out on your own, you will need to bear this in mind.

Roads are usually well signed, though in some out-of-the-way places, you may come across some intersections with no signage. Routes covered in this book will give you a clear direction in such cases. If you are exploring other routes, be sure to carry a recent map. You may find some of the signs rather intriguing, especially those with pictures of kangaroo, emus, or wombats, which are warning you to take care not to hit these animals. This is not really a problem on your bike, but they can cause an amazing amount of damage to fast-moving cars.

Chapter 6.
Preparing to Tour

Equipment: What You'll Need to Tour

If you already have a decent bike, setting yourself up for cycle touring requires minimal additional equipment. If you don't, you have the opportunity to purchase your ideal touring machine. A little time and extra money spent shopping around for quality gear appropriate for your needs will pay dividends in the future. Once you have made the initial investment in equipment, going cycle touring is as easy as pedaling out of your driveway.

The Ideal Touring Bike—Touring or Mountain Bike?

A suitable touring bike is critical to your overall comfort and enjoyment while touring. If you have a good bike already, then chances are you'll want to bring it with you. If you're new to bicycle touring and are considering to purchase a new bike for the purpose, you may find the following helpful.

In most cycle touring books, readers are discouraged from purchasing a mountain bike in favor of a dedicated touring

Loaded mountain bikes at Wrights bridge over the Blackwood River in Western Australia.

bike. This was probably good advice at the time these publications were written, because early in their development, mountain bikes were very heavy and generally unsuitable and cumbersome for all but the most demanding of touring situations. Now, however, with advances in design and the increasing use of lightweight materials, the difference in weight and maneuverability between high-quality touring bikes and mountain bikes is negligible, meaning that the choice is no longer so clear cut. On my travels, I have encountered many cyclists on both types of bike, and everyone seems to praise the virtues of his or her own particular machine. Much of it boils down to personal preference, although in my opinion, a mountain bike offers greater flexibility because of its greater ability to handle less than ideal conditions.

I should also stress at this point that you will usually have to make a couple of minor modifications to a mountain bike in order to make it suitable for touring. The fat, knobby tires that generally come as standard are great off-road but will slow you down considerably on the bitumen. The whirring sound they make as you ride along is an audible indication of the energy you are wasting trying to overcome friction between the tire and the road surface. These fat tires should be replaced by thinner, smoother tires designed for on-road use. They should be totally smooth (slicks) or have a hybrid pattern, the choice of which is really dependent on the surface conditions you are likely to encounter on your tour. If you are on sealed roads almost all the time, slicks are probably the best bet, whereas hybrids offer a compromise between on- and off-road performance when a certain amount of travel on unsealed roads is anticipated. You'll have to make a compromise that offers the best overall performance.

The second modification that you should make to your mountain bike is the addition of bar ends, although increasingly these are now fitted as standard equipment. Bar ends, as the name suggests, are small, curved metal bars that attach to the ends of the existing flat handlebars. They allow you to vary your hand position and also provide a more comfortable grip for climbing. Without them, after a while you are likely to experience pins and needles or numbness in your hands and arms because of the constant pressure exerted on certain nerves when restricted to just the one hand position.

Buying a Bike: What to Look For

Regardless of whether you opt for a mountain or touring bike, there are several points you should bear in mind when making a purchase. The first is to decide whether to buy your bike at home or get it once you arrive.

Buying at home will let you familiarize yourself with the bike and break it in. Bike shops generally tell you to bring your new bicycle in after a month or so to be adjusted, as nuts, bolts, and gears often slacken off after initial use. Also, if in the future you have to make a claim on your warranty, it's a lot easier if you can take your bike back to where you purchased it. On the down side, you have to carry your bike with you to Australia. Although with most airlines that is not a major problem, it may be inconvenient if you are also visiting a number of countries where you don't intend to cycle.

Purchasing your bike once you arrive is another option. There are plenty of good bike shops in all major cities, with a wide range of brands available, although specialized touring equipment may be more difficult to find. In terms of price, if you intend to purchase a bike at the higher end of the scale, it's likely that you'll find it more expensive than in North America or the UK, as many of them are imported from these regions. As a rough guide, you should be able to pick up a new bike suitable for touring from around $600.

How Good a Bike Do You Need?

Throughout my travels I've seen people touring on bikes of all descriptions, ranging from single-speed, iron-framed antiques to super-lightweight, super-expensive thoroughbreds that have left me drooling. The point is that you can tour on just about anything with two wheels, but an investment in a good, quality bike with suitable features for touring will pay dividends in terms of both comfort and reliability.

Look for a bike with three front chainrings (more or less standard on mountain bikes), giving you 21 or 24 gears to choose from. Although when riding around unladen you might find it difficult to imagine situations where you are ever likely to require the lowest ("granny") gears, you'll appreciate having them as you turn the pedals of your fully loaded bike up the last few km of a 10 km climb. Cantilever brakes, as opposed to caliper brakes, are also preferable, as they offer greater stopping power—an advantage when trying to slow a bike that is considerably heavier than normal.

In terms of componentry, bikes offering a complete integrated "gruppo" (group-set to my non-American readers) are usually best, as all the parts have been specifically designed to work well together. Also bear in mind the ease of getting suitable spare parts in foreign countries. In this respect, Shimano parts are more or less standard on most Australian bikes, and spares should be readily available in all bike shops. On the other hand, bikes with more exotic components may pose problems, especially in more remote areas.

If faced with a choice between a couple of similar models, one lighter and one with better components, go for the bike with the better components. Although weight is an important consideration, money is better spent on quality components, as once fully loaded, a bike that is a few grams lighter will offer no noticeable performance difference. Other small but worthwhile things to look for are braze-on mounts for two or three water bottle cages and a rear rack (often missing on aluminum bikes).

Finally, go to a bike shop that either specializes in touring or at least seems to know what it's on about, tell them your requirements and have them explain the various features of some suitable models.

Racks and Panniers

Panniers are the equivalent of backpacks for your bike and will carry most of your equipment on a tour. There are panniers designed to go on the front or rear of your bike, and bags to go on the handlebars. Which panniers you will need depends on the length and type of tour you are going to ride. As with most pursuits where you must carry all of your equipment, the general rule of thumb is, the less stuff to carry the better. Most of the time I try to use only rear panniers and a handlebar bag. If you're not carrying camping equipment and not getting too far off the beaten track, you should find that this combination offers ample room to carry all that you require. On extended tours in remote areas, you'll probably need to carry camping gear, lots of water, food, and spare parts, thus requiring the extra room provided by the addition of front panniers.

A handlebar bag is a very handy item for carrying things you will want ready access to throughout the day, such as your camera, guidebook, sunscreen, and food. Most handlebar bags also have a clear plastic map pocket on top, allowing you to navigate without having to stop. Bar bags are easy to remove and, with the addition of a shoulder strap, can be easily carried around off the bike, making them a good place to keep your valuables.

When buying panniers, it's worthwhile investing in quality equipment in order to save yourself some headaches later. Look for durable construction, functional design, and an easy attachment system. Also check out the warranty offered by the manufacturer. I personally use English-made Karrimor panniers, which have an excellent attachment system and a lifetime warranty, but there are plenty of good brands around made both by bike companies and by manufacturers of outdoor equipment. Take the time to shop around: a high-quality set of panniers should offer you many years of touring service.

Panniers attach to racks, or carriers, which in turn attach to the bike. Invest in a quality rack of durable construction that attaches securely to the frame. Most cyclists seem to agree that Blackburn makes a very good product.

Finally, a small backpack such as a schoolbag is also very useful. You can store things such as your sleeping bag in it, then fasten it to the rear rack with a bungee cord, giving you a considerable amount of extra space. Off the bike, the bag also comes in very handy as a day pack for carrying your gear when you walk around town.

Packing Panniers

Although it's likely you'll soon develop your own favorite system for packing your panniers, here are a few suggestions that may help.

Despite the manufacturers' claims, even the best panniers won't keep out all water. Therefore, it is essential to line the panniers with a waterproof liner before packing them (or more conveniently, pack your stuff in a plastic bag the same size as your pannier bag, and then put it in). You can buy bags specifically designed for the task from outdoor stores, although I find garbage bags work just as well. Make sure to pack a couple of spare bags, as they tear quite easily and also come in handy for many other uses.

For extra protection against water leakage and as a way of organizing your gear, ziplock bags can be very useful. It's always a good idea to keep at least one set of clothing in one, so you'll have something warm and dry to put on if other barriers against leakage fail. You can also store your dirty laundry in them.

Pack the panniers in a logical, systematic order, with similar items packed together. Put items you'll frequently require or will need to get at in a hurry (such as your raincoat) near the top, and items you'll only occasionally need (such as camp stoves) toward the bottom.

Try to balance the bike by making your left and right panniers approximately the same weight, and if using front panniers as well, distribute the load so that approximately 60% of the weight is on the back of the bike, and 40% on the front.

Bike Repairs

A major disaster is unlikely on a well-maintained bike. The most common problems you're likely to encounter are annoying flat tires and the occasional broken spoke. Therefore, unless you're venturing to some particularly remote area, you need carry only a fairly basic tool kit in order to overcome most problems.

Tools and Parts

- [ ] puncture repair kit

- [ ] tire levers—for removing the tire

- [ ] spare inner tube

- [ ] pump—make sure it matches your valve fitting. Schrader valves (the type also used on car tires) are a good idea, as in the absence of a pump, you can easily and effortlessly inflate your tires at any gas station.

- [ ] set of Allen wrenches—a multi-tool that looks like a pocket knife and has Allen wrenches and other bits and pieces is very useful, and should be available in your local bike shop.

- [ ] small adjustable wrench—for removing pedals at the airport and for other adjustments

- [ ] 3 or 4 spare spokes—make sure they are the right length for your wheels.

- [ ] roll of strong adhesive tape—good for all sorts of running repairs

- [ ] lubricant—a teflon-based product specifically designed for bikes is preferable to conventional mineral oil.

- [ ] crank extractor—for tightening the cranks if they start coming loose

- [ ] rear cluster removal tool—for removing the rear cluster so you can change spokes on the rear wheel yourself (where breakages will occur nine times out of ten)

- [ ] spare tire—probably a wise precaution, especially if you anticipate a lot of off-road travel

A broken spoke is no major drama but can cause severe buckling of your wheel if left unattended for too long. If you are unsure how to change tires or replace spokes, visit your local bike shop and ask the mechanic to show you how to do it. Usually he will be happy to help. If in doubt about how to fix something, where possible get a bike shop to attend to your repairs.

Touring Accessories

Bike computer

A bike computer is an extremely useful touring accessory. It will help you to navigate by letting you know how far you've traveled and how far you've got to go. It will also keep a running tally of the distance you've covered (I always have a mini-celebration every time another 1000 km clicks over on the odometer). Most also tell you your speed, maximum speed, average speed, cycling time, trip distance, and local time.

Helmet

As well as being compulsory now in all Australian states, wearing a helmet makes good sense. Lightweight and constantly improving in their appearance, helmets offer life-saving protection. If you've never worn one before, you'll soon get used to it.

Gloves

In a fall you always stick out your hands to cushion the impact. Gloves ensure that a minor spill isn't any more painful than it has to be, by protecting you against dreaded gravel rash. Some gloves with gel inserts in the palms also cushion you from the vibration transferred from the road through the handlebars. Finally, gloves provide sun protection for the back of your hands, an area that I painfully found to be particularly susceptible to sunburn while cycling.

Water bottles and water bags

Australia can be very dry and very hot, particularly in summer. Therefore, in order to remain hydrated you need to carry plenty of water (please refer to section on water precautions on page 34). I usually carry two large water bottles in the bottle cages on my bike, as well as a 4-liter water bag on my rear rack. Water bags can be purchased from outdoor stores. In addition to their large capacities, one of the biggest advantages of a bag over additional bottles is that when not in use, a bag folds away to almost nothing, saving valuable space in your panniers.

Front and rear lights

You should never plan to ride in the dark, but for one reason or another you may have to from time to time. Therefore, it is important that you carry lights, especially a good rear light, so that you are clearly visible. A decent front light will also double as a handy torch around camp.

Compass

A small compass is a handy item. Country roads are often unmarked, meaning you may be occasionally uncertain of which one to take. A compass in conjunction with a map will ensure that you make the right choice.

Bike lock

Nothing can ruin your holiday worse than having your bike stolen, particularly if your panniers are still attached to it; it is essential to have a sturdy lock to secure your bike whenever it is out of your sight. U-locks, such as those made by Kryptonite, offer the best level of protection, and although quite heavy, they are still the way to go. I secure the rear wheel and frame to an immovable object with a U-lock, then use a second cable-type lock to fasten the front wheel to the frame. If traveling with a companion it's a good idea to exchange sets of spare keys so that if your set is misplaced you don't have to chase up a pair of bolt cutters.

Camping Equipment

Carrying camping gear gives you the freedom to go wherever you want without worrying about where to stay and gives you access to what is often the cheapest form of accommodation. On the down side, camping gear will add considerably to the amount of equipment you have to carry. If you think that you will use it infrequently, it's probably best to leave it at home. If you do plan on camping, don't forget to pack a fuel stove, as open fires are banned in many areas because of the fire risk.

Buying Camping Equipment and Outdoor Gear in Australia

There are some excellent manufacturers of high-quality outdoor gear in Australia, with companies such as Mountain Designs and Paddy Pallin outfitting many prominent adventurers. Specialist suppliers like these cater to the top end of the market and can be quite expensive, although generally the investment in quality is worthwhile. You can usually find more reasonably priced gear in army surplus stores.

There is a tendency for outdoor stores to be clustered tightly together in Australian cities, making it easy to wander from one shop to the next to compare gear and prices. Outdoor stores are probably the best places to look for panniers.

Clothes for Cycling

The type of clothes you should pack depends largely on the time of year and the parts of the country you'll be visiting (see climate information section). Bear in mind that panniers offer only a limited amount of space, especially if carrying camping equipment, so you should give careful thought to the clothes you bring to ensure that infrequently used items aren't needlessly carried around. Less is definitely best, but at the same time your comfort should not be sacrificed for the sake of saving a few grams.

Cycling shorts with a padded chamois in the crotch are pretty much essential to prevent becoming sore from long periods in the saddle. I usually wear a lightweight pair of shorts over the top of mine as well, for a couple of reasons. First, I find it handy to have access to some pockets during the day, and second, it makes you a little less conspicuous when walking around town. On top I generally just wear a t-shirt, or a lightweight, long-sleeve shirt with a high collar, to prevent sunburn in hot weather. In cooler conditions, I sometimes wear a warm jacket, such as one made of Polartech fleece, when starting out in the morning.

A rain jacket is also handy when the heavens open, although often the sweat collected inside the jacket makes you just as uncomfortable as being rained on. Gore-Tex fabric solves this problem to a degree, but still traps perspiration during heavy exertion. Try to get a raincoat specifically designed for cycling. They are cut low in the front to allow freedom of movement, and long in the back to protect against spray, and for safety reasons usually come in highly visible colors. Waterproof leggings aren't really necessary unless conditions are extreme. If you anticipate cold conditions, a set of thermal underwear layered with other items of clothing offers effective, lightweight warmth.

Although cycling shoes specifically designed for touring are available, a comfortable, sturdy pair of sneakers does just fine, and saves you from having to carry an extra pair to wear off the bike. Shoes made of leather offering some level of water protection are ideal and should be treated with a waterproofing agent such as Snowseal on a regular basis to maximize their performance.

Sunglasses are also important items, not only to protect against the often very bright Australian sun but also to guard the eyes against debris and insects when cycling along, especially when going downhill at high speed.

Off the Bike

The amount of clothing you'll need to bring for wear off the bike is obviously largely dependent on the kind of places you intend to visit. If you are traveling on a budget you're unlikely to require a coat and tie or formal dress, but it's advisable to take a respectable set of clothing for going out at night. Bring an ample supply of underwear and socks, maybe 3 or 4 pairs of each, as they weigh little and will save you from doing your laundry too often.

Other items you'll need or that are highly recommended include a swimsuit, towel, toiletries, basic first aid kit, Swiss Army knife, sunscreen, compass, flashlight (torch to non-American readers), spare batteries, and your camera. Don't bring regular bath towels, as they are too bulky and take too long to dry. If possible, get a chamois-type travel towel. Although not as luxurious to use, they are quite effective, dry much faster, and take up a lot less room in your luggage. As a bit of a luxury item, I also carry a small short-wave radio to fill in some of those quiet hours and catch up on the news while in small country towns and other places where recreational activities are somewhat limited.

Transporting Your Bike

By air

Airlines generally count a bike as part of your general luggage allowance, which for economy class is usually 20 kg. As your bike probably weighs between 10 and 12 kg, you don't have much weight to spare, so you have to be careful about what you carry as hand luggage. Pack all your heaviest and most valuable items into one pannier and carry it aboard the aircraft with you. This should bring you within your allowance, but if it doesn't, don't get overly concerned. Many airlines I have flown on have shown little concern about a few kg here or there, although you do occasionally hear stories about people being penalized for being only a few grams over. If you do go significantly over the limit, you will have to pay an excess luggage charge.

Airline policy differs as to whether you are required to pack your bike in a box, although this is probably a good idea anyway to prevent damage. Wrapping your sleeping bag around the bike (after wrapping greasy parts to protect your bag) when in the box is also not a bad idea, as it provides additional padding and frees up space in your other luggage.

To fit your bike in a box, you will usually have to remove the front wheel, turn the handlebars parallel with the frame, lower your seat, and remove your pedals. These are all fairly simple procedures, and with a little practice it should take you only about 10 minutes or so to reassemble the bike once you arrive. (But do practice at home using the tools you will take with you, to make sure you can do it.) If you are nervous about the effect of the reduced air pressure in the cargo hold, you can play it safe by letting some air out of the tires.

By train

On suburban commuter trains, you can carry your bike with you, although in some cities, such as Brisbane, you must ride in a designated carriage. Sometimes you will also have to pay for your bike, usually the equivalent of a concession fare. Check when you buy your ticket.

On interstate and country trains, bike policy varies depending on the type of train used. On long-haul and old-style trains, such as the Indian Pacific, your bike is carried in the baggage car, boxed or unboxed, at additional expense. This is also the case for Victoria country services.

On modern high-speed trains, such as the XPT that runs between Sydney and Brisbane, the bicycle policy is even more restrictive. Apparently, in the absence of a baggage car, there is only room for two bikes per train, so you have to reserve a place for your bike, which has to be boxed, before the train leaves the first station of its journey.

Buses

Suburban buses do not take bikes, although I have heard of plans to introduce some with bike-carrying facilities in the future.

Long-distance coach companies, such as Greyhound, will carry bikes at an additional charge, usually requiring partial disassembly.

Symbols used in the route maps in Chapters 7–14

🏕	Youth Hostel (YHA)
▲	Campground
▬▬▬▬	Road (route highlighted)
▬ ▬ ▬ ▬	Unsealed road (route highlighted)
═══════	Freeway, divided highway (route highlighted)
━┿━┿━■━┿━	Railway with station

Chapter 7.
Adelaide to Melbourne

This is a long but generally easy route, taking in a wealth of varied sights in two states. The tour takes in Adelaide, the city of churches; the renowned wine-producing Barossa Valley; the mighty Murray River; the pristine Coorong National Park; and spectacular Victoria coastline, including the world famous Great Ocean Road, ending in Melbourne.

If you are short on time, you can easily ride the Great Ocean Road section of the tour separately, making for an unforgettable 4 or 5 days cycling. To do this shorter tour, catch a train to Warrnambool from Melbourne's Spencer St. station.

Southern Ocean swells and blustery breezes batter the coast near Loch Ard Gorge.

Start	Adelaide, North Terrace
Finish	Geelong, to ride in to Melbourne by train
Distance	1,194 km (740 miles)
Duration	3 weeks, 16 cycling days
Terrain	This route mainly follows the coast and is predominantly flat, with the exception of the Otway ranges on the Great Ocean Road.
Road Conditions	Traffic is fairly light on the bulk of the route, although it starts to get busier as you approach Melbourne on the Great Ocean Road. Quite a lot of riding is done on the Princes Highway, which thankfully is nowhere near as busy as you might expect, carrying very little traffic most of the time. There are only a few sections of unsealed road to endure, all of them found along the Murray River section of the tour.
Accomm.	Motels, pubs, and campgrounds. There are also several youth hostels along the route.

Adelaide

Adelaide, often referred to as the "city of churches," could just as easily be called the city of parks. The city center is ringed by them, making Adelaide a most attractive city to explore by bike or on foot. The city was founded in 1836 by William Light, who proclaimed the area a British colony and named it Adelaide after his wife.

The city is laid out in an easily navigable grid pattern. The main thoroughfare runing north-south is King William St. Streets running east-west change their names as they cross King William St. There is a long pedestrian mall in Rundle St., flanked by the usual assortment of department stores and specialty shops, as well as some good cafes and outdoor stores at the eastern end, which is open to traffic. Hindley St. is the center of much of Adelaide's night life, with a good selection of restaurants, pubs, and night clubs in the area. Most of the city's public buildings, such as the art gallery, library, museum, Government House, and the University of Adelaide, are situated on North Terrace, as is the Adelaide casino. Behind North Terrace, meandering through leafy parkland is the river Torrens, separating the city from North

Adelaide, an older area full of interesting pubs, restaurants, and expensive shops. The Adelaide Oval, Australia's prettiest cricket ground, and St. Mary's cathedral are also close to the river, which has a nice cycle path running alongside it.

If the weather is good, take a trip out to Glenelg, home to one of Adelaide's most popular beaches as well as a number of other attractions. Getting there, as they say, is half the fun; Adelaide's only tram will take you there, departing regularly from Victoria Square in the city center and taking about half an hour to complete the journey.

In addition to its numerous up-market hotels, Adelaide also has a good selection of budget accommodation, including many backpacker establishments. The YHA hostel is in the southeast corner of town, along with quite a few other hostels, at 290 Gilles St. There are also a few backpacker places located near the central bus station on Franklin St., as well as by the beach in Glenelg.

Day 1   Adelaide to Kersbrook YHA
half day (50 km/31 miles)

Unlike Sydney and Melbourne, where I recommend you catch a train out of the city, leaving Adelaide on a bike is a rather pleasant and civilized experience. A bike path runs alongside the river Torrens for quite some distance, and although the route can be confusing at times—the path tends to end abruptly in places, only to continue on the other side of the river— it's hard to go wrong if you stick next to the Torrens.

A convenient and central place to pick up the path is just behind the picturesque University of Adelaide on North Terrace. Once on the path, cycle upstream through tranquil, leafy parkland, leaving the city of Adelaide behind you. Along the way you pass under a number of traffic and busway (a bus running on concrete rails) bridges. After passing under several of these bridges, you pass under a traffic bridge, then a busway bridge in quick succession, encountering another traffic bridge about 1 km later, which is the Lower North East Rd. Turn right to leave the cycle path at this point (it ends soon anyway). Turning left off Lower North East Rd. onto George St., a suburban road running parallel with the river. George St. eventually turns into Lower Athelstone Rd. and after a km or two terminates at Coullis Rd. A right turn brings you out to Gorge Rd.

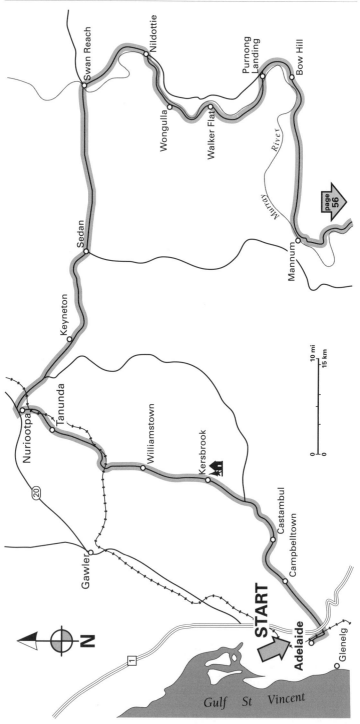

Having turned left onto Gorge Rd., navigation becomes somewhat easier, and it's not long before you can see why the roads bears its name. Traffic is surprisingly light, making for an enjoyable cycling experience as you follow the path of the ever-narrowing river, sheer rock walls towering above either side of the road. After approximately 30 km, you pass through Castambul before encountering a fairly significant climb that takes you past the Kangaroo Creek reservoir. There are some nice views out across the dam as you climb, giving your mind something else to appreciate besides the pain in your legs. A short distance later you come to Cudlee Creek, where apart from a general store, a pub, and a caravan park, there's also a wildlife park. If you've yet to encounter some of Australia's native fauna, it's probably worth stopping in for a look, although I can almost guarantee that by the time you finish this tour, you will have seen kangaroos and emus in the wild anyway. Just beyond Cudlee Creek, turn left onto a road signed to Williamstown. This road soon joins another busier road that forks a short distance later. Take the left fork, signed to Williamstown and Kersbrook (5 km), to conclude the first day of the tour.

Kersbrook is only a small place but possesses the essentials for small town life: general store, post office, and pub. Accommodation options are fairly limited. You can stay at a guest house located next to the general store, although the best choice is probably the small YHA hostel situated about 2 km out of town in the direction of Williamstown. There's no resident caretaker, so you have to arrange to pick up the key from the key holder, who at the time of writing lives in a house on the right side of the road about 400 m before the hostel, opposite Wattle Rd. The hostel itself is a small, white building located on the left-hand side of the road in a rural setting next to a farm dam. It's only just visible from the road. You have to go through a small gate (unfriendly to bikes) and walk a few hundred meters down a track to get to it.

Day 2   *Kersbrook to Nuriootpa*
half day (40 km/25 miles)

This is a short, easy ride, allowing you plenty of time to experience the charms of the Barossa Valley, as well as giving you the opportunity to take part in a wine-tasting session at one or more of the numerous vineyards that dot the area. From Kersbrook, head out along the fairly flat and lightly trafficked road to Williamstown, which lies 15 km away. Just before reaching the town, you'll spot the first vines of many for the day. Turning left at Williamstown, the road continues 8 km to Lyndoch. A sign by the road marks your arrival in the Barossa Valley. From Lyndoch, turn right after crossing the railway tracks on the way into town, on to the Tanunda Road. The traffic on this 13 km stretch of road increases a little with the addition of tourist traffic and winery trucks heading for Tanunda, the most Germanic and popular of the Barossa towns. The rolling road passes by a fine example of an old Lutheran church at Rowland Flat and crosses Jacob's Creek, an ordinary-looking waterway that lends its name to one of Australia's most popular wines.

Tanunda itself is a pleasant little town reflecting the German heritage of the district. Some examples of early cottages can be seen around Goat Square. The main street is dotted with cafes, restaurants, and various other shops, including the Barossa visitors center, which is well worth a visit if you're in need of some information about the area. Just out of Tanunda, pick up the cycle path, which provides a pleasant traffic-free ride for the final 7 km into Nuriootpa.

Nuriootpa, situated on the North Para River, is the commercial center of the Barossa Valley. Various accommodation options are available in town. For the budget traveler I recommend a stay at the Barossa Bunkhaus, a hostel set among the vines, situated on the right side of the road about a km short of the town itself.

Day 3   *Nuriootpa to Swan Reach*
(68 km/42 miles)

Today's ride leaves the Barossa behind as you head to join one of Australia's great rivers, the Murray. After passing the stately buildings of the Penfold winery on your left, as you come into Nuriootpa, cross the railway lines, then turn right down the road signposted to Angaston. There are good views back down the valley as the road gently climbs the Barossa ranges, bringing you to Angaston at the 7 km point. The town itself is very pleasant, boasting a couple of nice parks and some fine examples of colonial architecture.

Continue up Angaston's main street, turning right at the end and following the road signed to Keyneton. A short distance on, the road forks. Take the left fork, signed to Swan Reach. Leaving Angaston, the countryside begins to change, becoming open grazing land, which in summer takes on a brown, parched appearance. The trees lining this lightly trafficked road host a variety of bird life including brightly colored rosellas, pink and grey galahs, and magpies. At the 18 km point you come to the hamlet of Keyneton. There's not a lot here, but the general store provides a welcome opportunity to purchase a cold drink.

From Keyneton, after some straight stretches of road and climbs up long, gentle slopes, you reach the top of Sedan Hill at the 26 km mark. This point offers fine views over the plain below, and the "Steep Descent" sign by the roadside signals that there's some easy cycling ahead. Sit back and enjoy the fruits of your labor as you freewheel a good part of the remaining 11 km to Sedan. The town is very small, but there's a pub and a supermarket, where food for lunch is available. Make sure to fill your water bottles here, as the remainder of the route to Swan Reach can be very hot and dry, with little protection from the sun.

From Sedan, continue ahead on the road signed to Swan Reach. The next 31 km are along a very straight, flat and quiet road, traveling through mallee scrubland. The Murray River is a welcome sight as you approach Swan Reach. A ferry, operating 24 hours a day, will take you across the river and into the town. Pub-style accommodation is available at the Swan Reach hotel, situated next to the ferry landing, or you can camp at the caravan park over to the right.

Day 4   Swan Reach to Mannum
(86 km/54 miles)

The route from Swan Reach to Mannum follows the mighty Murray downstream over flat terrain on a variety of road surfaces. Turn right from the ferry landing and cycle past the caravan park on the road to Nildottie, then turn right again about 1 km later at a T-junction, on to the road signed to Walker Flat and Mannum. After 10 km, you come across a lookout and picnic area, providing a good view of the sheer cliffs that are a feature of this section of river. Nildottie, at 14 km, has little more than a general store, and after passing another lookout, you arrive at the turnoff to Walker's Flat at the 29 km point. Here the sealed road ends as you ignore the turnoff and continue straight ahead toward Purnong.

The surface quality of this stretch may vary greatly depending on recent weather conditions, amount of use, and

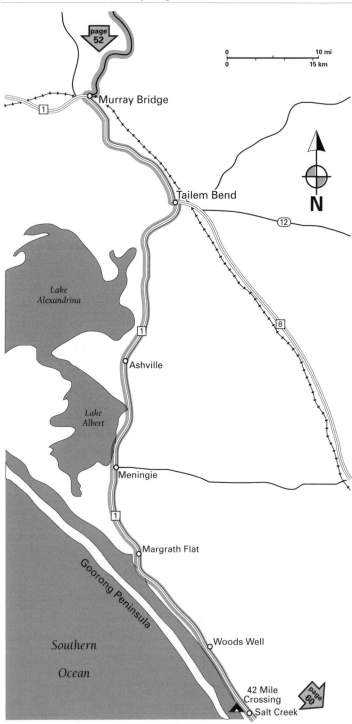

page
52

0   10 mi
0   15 km

N

Murray Bridge

1

Tailem Bend

12

8

Lake Alexandrina

1

Ashville

Lake Albert

Meningie

1

Southern

Ocean

Goorong Peninsula

Margrath Flat

Woods Well

42 Mile Crossing
Salt Creek

page
60

the time since it was last graded, but when I rode it, apart from corrugations in places, it wasn't too bad. At the 41 km mark, you pass the turnoff to Purnong, continuing ahead through open mallee scrub still on the unsealed surface. After 52 km there's a welcome opportunity to turn off to the right, take a break, and grab a cold drink at the small settlement of Bowhill. This road is a dead end, so you'll have to backtrack a km or so, but the chance to relax for a while in the shade on the banks of the Murray should be a sufficient incentive.

After getting back on the main route, the unsealed stretch continues for about another 8 km, after which the sight of bitumen is bound to be a gratifying. After a short, luxurious section of sealed road, you come to an intersection at the 60 km mark, where you are faced with a decision. If you turn right, the route follows the river the remaining 27 km to Mannum. This is the scenic option, but the bulk of the way is unsealed. If you can't possibly face any more dirt road, continue ahead along the slightly shorter sealed route.

After 86 km, hop aboard a ferry and travel across to Mannum. This is a sizeable town, once the cradle of river trade along the Murray. The P.S. *Marion*, an example of a typical river boat, lies moored next to the tourist information office just to the left of the ferry landing. Your accommodation options here include the Mannum motel or the caravan park, which has some of the nicest tent sites I've seen, both situated adjacent to the ferry. There is also a free camping area with limited facilities on the other side of the river. Just continue past the ferry to the end of the road. It's pretty primitive, but the price is right.

Day 5   Mannum to Murray Bridge
half day (48 km/30 miles)

Cycle up Mannum's main street, passing the war memorial (a feature of almost every Australian town), before turning left at a crossroad by a gas station. This road takes you past the golf course, after which it becomes unsealed for a few km, passing between dairy farms before rejoining the main road. Turn left, and a short while after crossing the Reedy Creek bridge, turn left again on the small sealed road to Caloote. After a while, the road is unsealed, and after passing through Caloote you eventually come to a point where the road forks at a concrete water tank. Take the right fork and turn right again at the bottom of the hill, traveling past the collection of houses called Wall Flat. Turn right at a T-junction, and after traveling a short distance, turn left down the road signed to Mypalonga. Eventually the road comes out near an orchard, where it becomes sealed; turn left here down to a grassed area by the river known as Woodlane Reserve. Taking a right by the reserve, cycle along a flat, small unsealed road that winds its way through the reeds by the river, passing through a mixture of orchards and dairy farms. Follow this road until eventually you come to a "no through road" sign, where you turn right and climb a short, steep hill, rejoining the sealed surface at the top. Turn left, then left again at a T-junction a short distance later, following this road all the way to Murray Bridge. The traffic increases as you approach the town, although it is still fairly light. After crossing some railway lines on the outskirts, pick up the cycle path for the final couple of km.

Murray Bridge is the largest of the river towns, so as you would expect there is a range of accommodation alternatives available. I would highly recommend the Balcony hotel, located in the center of town. It's clean and cheap and has friendly, helpful owners. Murray Bridge has regular bus services to Adelaide and is also located on the main Adelaide-Melbourne rail line.

Day 6   *Murray Bridge to Meningie*
                       (84 km/52 miles)

Leave Murray Bridge via the main road you came in on, passing under the freeway overpass a few km later. If you're interested, there's a butterfly house and puzzle park located here. Follow the road 34 km to Wellington, passing through dairy pastures that look decidedly more fertile and lush than those farther north. At Wellington there's an old courthouse, which is now a museum and is well worth a visit while you're waiting for the ferry to come and take you across the river for the final time.

Once across the river, continue for a short distance before joining the Princes Highway. Although in planning the rides for this book I have endeavored to avoid highways where possible, I'm afraid that in this part of the country there isn't a lot of choice. Anyway, it's really not bad; the traffic is surprisingly light, as the bulk of commuter and truck traffic uses the more direct Dukes Highway on its way to Melbourne. Turn right at the highway and follow it the remaining 44 km to Meningie. The width and quality of the shoulder varies, although it is generally quite good. You can tell you're getting closer to the ocean as the scenery turns to coastal scrub interspersed with salt lakes, and if you're unlucky as I was, the wind howls in your face.

Meningie, situated on the shores of Lake Albert, is the gateway to the Coorong National Park. In town you can stay at the motel, pub, or caravan park.

The Coorong National Park stretches some 145 km (90 miles) from the mouth of the Murray River to just north of the town of Kingston. The huge sand dunes of the Younghusband Peninsula separate the salty Coorong inland sea from the Southern Ocean. The area is renowned for its flora and fauna, especially the many varieties of water birds that call the area home. Camping is allowed throughout the park, but you have to buy a permit from the national park offices at Meningie and Salt Creek, or at a gas station along the way. To fully appreciate the area you really have to get off the highway and over to the Younghusband Peninsula. Organized tours depart regularly from Meningie.

Day 7   Meningie to 42 Mile Crossing Camping Area
(78 km/49 miles)

Apart from camping, there is no accommodation available at 42 Mile Crossing. The last fixed accommodation prior to Kingston is located at Policeman's Point (48 km/30 miles).

Continue along the Princes Highway out of Meningie, entering the Coorong National Park about 24 km (15 miles) later. From MacGrath Flat, the road skirts the edge of the Coorong inland sea, with the Younghusband Peninsula visible beyond. There's a caravan park and kiosk at Wood's Well (40 km/25 miles), and a motel, caravan park, and roadhouse 8 km farther up the road at Policeman's Point. A replica oil rig stands by the side of the road at Salt Creek at the 59 km point, a monument to the first oil well drilled in Australia, which never actually found oil. In addition to a couple of roadhouses, there's a national parks office at Salt Creek. If you're not camping at 42 Mile Crossing (water available from tank), make sure to fill your water bottles here, as there's no more until Kingston.

The turnoff to 42 Mile Crossing is at the 75 km point on the right side of the road. The camping area is situated about 3 km down a dirt road. There are toilet facilities, a shelter, and

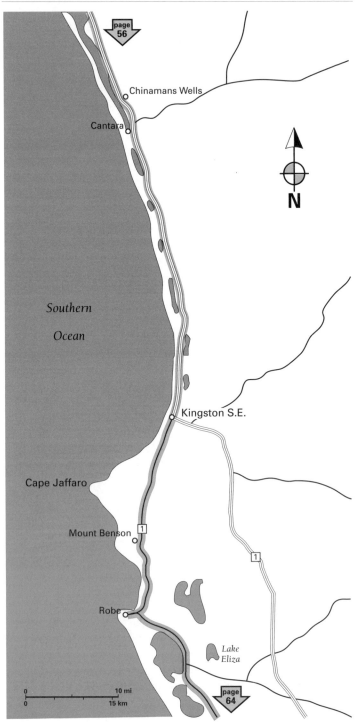

page 56

Chinamans Wells

Cantara

Southern

Ocean

Kingston S.E.

Cape Jaffaro

Mount Benson [1]

Robe

[1]

Lake Eliza

N

0   10 mi
0   15 km

page 64

rain water. Named 42 Mile Crossing because of its distance from Kingston, it is the only all-weather, all-year crossing point over to the Younghusband Peninsula. It's about a 20-minute walk over the dunes to get to the beach.

Day 8   42 Mile Crossing to Kingston
(71 km/44 miles)

Once back on the Princes Highway it's a fairly easy 68 km to the small beach resort of Kingston. However, the flat, open terrain can leave you exposed to an often less than favorable wind. One of the first things you see as you approach the town is the looming presence of Larry the Lobster, a giant, bright orange tribute to the local crayfish industry. For some reason, an increasing number of Australian towns have felt the need to erect oversize and often terrible likenesses of local flora and fauna. As awful as they are, they seem to instill in me an overpowering urge to get out my camera and fire away, evidenced by my growing photo collection of "big" Australian landmarks. Some of the ones you'll come across on other tours in this book include the "Big Banana," the "Big Merino," and the "Big Trout," to name a few. Turn right shortly after a sign reading "Larry" to get to the main part of town. Various forms of accommodation are available here, the budget options being a backpacker's called Kingston Bunkers, on Holland St., or the caravan park located down on the waterfront.

Day 9   Kingston to Beachport
(95 km/59 miles)

From Kingston, the route skirts the coast following alternative Highway 1, rejoining the Princes Highway at Millicent. There are a few small hills on the way to Robe, but nothing to get concerned about. Patches of pine plantation around Mt. Benson make for a nice change in scenery and act as a welcome windbreak if luck is against you. The coastal community of Robe lies about 3 km off the main route, and is a great place to rest for a while. There are some nice old buildings, including Customs House, built in 1863, as well as some good places to have lunch. If you feel like staying there's a range of accommodation available including the Robe backpacker's on Victoria St.

From Robe, get back out onto alternative Highway 1 and head for Beachport. This flat 52 km stretch of road passes by a string of lakes including Lake Eliza, Lake St. Clair, and Lake George. Like Robe, Beachport lies about 3 km off the main route. On the way into town you'll cycle past some nice surfing and swimming beaches, which may prove hard to resist at the end of a warm day.

A whaling port in its early days, Beachport boasts one of the longest jetties in South Australia. Stretching out into beautiful Rivoli Bay, it's right next to the superbly located youth hostel. I would recommend phoning ahead if you're planning on staying here, as it's one of the dropping-off points for the adventure bus companies that ply the route between Adelaide and Melbourne. There's nothing worse than arriving at a hostel, exhausted from a challenging day's cycling, only to find that some bus group has snapped up all the beds. If it's full, don't despair. Beachport also has a motel, a hotel, and a caravan park.

Day 10   Beachport to Mt. Gambier
(88 km/55 miles)

Continue on alternative Highway 1, which skirts Rivoli Bay before rejoining the Princes Highway 37 km later at Millicent. Millicent is an attractive and sizeable place boasting a swimming lake, nice parks, and a good variety of shops on its main street. Cycle down the main street following the road signed to Mt. Gambier.

Once back on the Princes Highway, the traffic increases noticeably, although it remains fairly light. A few km out of town, you pass by a paper mill on the right side of the road. Just beyond here you have a choice of routes depending on which local attraction you wish to see. Continue straight ahead along the highway and you'll come to the Tantanoola caves. Tours of the small but beautiful caves run on the hour and last about 25 minutes. If nothing else, the cool climate inside the chamber feels wonderful on a hot day. If taxidermy is more your scene, turn right and into the town of Tantanoola in order to see the Tantanoola tiger, displayed in the appropriately named Tantanoola Tiger hotel. The creature is actually an Assyrian wolf that was shot in 1895 after escaping from a shipwreck. After Tantanoola, continue straight ahead, rejoining the highway just beyond the caves.

After the caves, the road passes through some large pine plantations as you wind your way toward Mt. Gambier. Approaching the town, your eyes puzzle over the strangely shaped hill in the distance. This landform is actually the extinct volcano on which the town is built and from which it takes its name. Mt. Gambier is the largest town in the region, with a population of about 20,000. Its main attraction is the spectacular Blue Lake. This crater lake inexplicably turns an incredibly vivid shade of blue in November each year, assuming a less spectacular appearance again in March.

There are a couple of nice campgrounds up near the lake, but getting there involves a steep climb out of town. A wide range of accommodation is available in town, and although there isn't a true backpacker's, the Blue Lake motel on Kennedy Ave., just off the highway at the far end of town, has some dorm-style rooms at a reasonable price.

Day 11 Mt. Gambier to Mt. Richmond Youth Hostel (67 km/42 miles)

Head east out of Mt. Gambier along Commercial St., turning right on to the road signed to Nelson. This rolling road passes through a pleasant mixture of dairy pastures and pine forests as it leads you out of South Australia and across the Victoria border. Traffic is pretty light, although unfortunately the bulk of what there is consists mainly of logging trucks and dairy tankers.

The small town of Nelson, 37 km from Mt. Gambier, is nestled on the Glenelg River. It is sandwiched between the Lower Glenelg National Park and Discovery Bay Coastal Park, and numerous off-bike opportunities beckon. Hire a canoe, wet a fishing line, go for a walk, or take one of the cruise boats offering trips up the river to the Princess Margaret Rose caves.

Continue out of Nelson on the Nelson-Portland road, traveling through pockets of national park and extensive pine plantations. The peace and tranquility of your surroundings are shattered at regular intervals by the sound of semi-trailers bearing down from behind. Fortunately, most truck drivers will give you a fairly wide berth, although there always seems to be one who enjoys forcing you into the dirt. Just prior to Mt. Richmond there's a nice lookout offering great views over the pines to the ocean, known in these parts as the Shipwreck Coast.

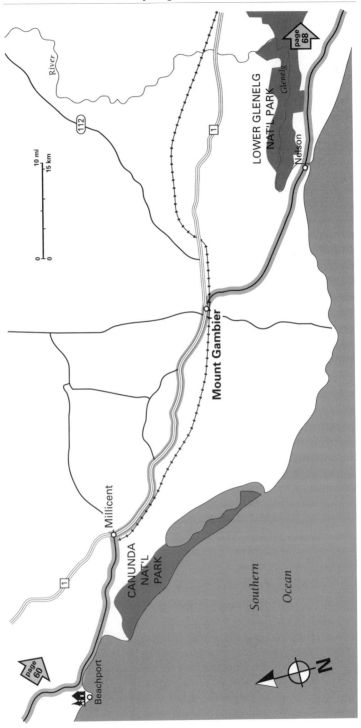

On the left side of the road, not far from the lookout, is the entrance to Nioka Farm (Mt. Richmond) youth hostel. Part of a working sheep farm, the hostel has a great homey feel. A hearty home-cooked dinner and breakfast are included in the overnight tariff. Make sure to book ahead, as there are only six beds available.

Day 12   Mt. Richmond Youth Hostel to Port Fairy
(110 km/68 miles)

Today's ride may sound a little daunting at 110 km, but with favorable winds the predominantly flat route shouldn't be too tough. If you have the time, reward yourself with a rest day or two in the great little town of Port Fairy.

Back out on the road, follow the signs to Portland. The road rolls along between state forest and pine plantations as it did yesterday. Toward Portland the route gets a little confusing. Ignore the road leading away to the right signed to the port and Smelter, and continue ahead over some railway lines, passing (and smelling) an abattoir on the right. At about the 37 km point, you come out on to the main road. If it's time for lunch or you just want to take a break, turn right and follow the road for a couple of km into the sizeable town of Portland. If you're keen to press on, turn right and then left shortly after, down a road called the Dutton Way.

The route meanders along the shore of Portland Bay for about 6 km, passing an assortment of holiday shacks and caravan parks. At the 43 km mark, turn left down a road signed to Warrnambool, which runs a short distance before bringing you back to an old friend, Highway 1, the Princes Highway. Turning right at the highway, it's not long before you come to the small outpost of Narrawong, where there's a general store and not much else. I remember huddling in a bus shelter here for an hour or so, trying to avoid the rain that had started the previous night and didn't let up all day. I hope the sun is shining for you. Anyway, the highway takes you all the way to Port Fairy, passing through a couple more small towns along the way. The road passes through farmland and is more or less flat and straight. The traffic, though fast, shouldn't be too heavy.

Eventually, after a long day (especially with headwinds), you come to the turnoff to Port Fairy, which is on your right. Port Fairy is one of the earliest settlements in the state of Victoria, dating back to 1835. The historical flavor of this small coastal town has been preserved with over 50 buildings classified by the National Trust, including the youth hostel. To get to the hostel, turn right onto Sackville St., which I guess could be called the main street (look for the YHA symbol on the street sign). Head along Sackville St., then turn left by the post office onto Cox St. The hostel, a nice one, is on the left a hundred meters or so down the road. Motel, B&B, and pub accommodation is also available. Although small, Port Fairy has a great atmosphere, with enough attractions to occupy a couple of leisurely days. My intended overnight stay ended up lasting three. In March make sure to book accommodation well in advance if possible, as the annual folk festival sees the town inundated with visitors.

Day 13   *Port Fairy to Port Campbell via Warrnambool* (94 km/ 58 miles)

Note: Great Ocean Road Ride

If you wish to do only the Great Ocean Road portion of this ride, Warrnambool is your starting point. Train services run daily from Melbourne's Spencer St. station to the town.

Head out of town and back onto the Princes Highway, turning right, in the direction of Warrnambool. After about 12 km, you encounter a bit of a climb at a place called Tower Hill. An extinct volcano, Tower Hill is now a reserve with some nice views and picnic areas. Keep an eye on thieving emus, who are only too happy to relieve you of a packed lunch. The road winds and rolls its way the next 14 km to Warrnambool, a provincial city with about 25,000 inhabitants, overlooking picturesque Lady Bay. If you arrive between July and October you may be fortunate enough to see the southern right whales that migrate every year from Antarctica to bear their young at a place called Logan's Beach.

Stay on the highway out of town, coming to a turnoff on the right after about 9 km, marked with a large sign saying "Great Ocean Road." After a short while you pass through Allansford, which has a cheese factory. If you like cheese, you'll be happy to hear that in addition to offering factory tours, they have over 100 types of Australian cheese for sale. Cycle along past dairy farms (no doubt supplying the cheese factory) and pass through the town of Nullawarre. Just as you start to think that there's not a lot of water to see on the Great Ocean Road, you hit the coast just before Peterborough at a place called the Bay of Islands. Powerful Southern Ocean swells, sheer eroded cliffs, and craggy limestone outcrops provide a spectacular introduction to the coast. The temptation to exhaust an entire roll of film is strong, but show some restraint, because over the next couple of days you'll encounter many more magnificent vantage points.

Petersborough is a small, unremarkable sort of place, its chief attraction being its proximity to the numerous formations in the area. Motel and caravan park accommodation is available.

From Petersborough the road hugs the coast, passing many more spectacular formations before bringing you to one of the better-known ones, a few km short of Port Campbell. London Bridge is a giant stone archway that until recently was connected to the mainland. It collapsed in 1990, leaving stranded several sightseers who had wandered across. Eventually, a nice freewheeling descent brings you to Port Campbell.

Port Campbell, which lies at the edge of a pretty little harbor, is one of the more popular holiday towns along the coast, so book ahead in summer. The youth hostel is situated opposite the caravan park and near the national parks office, where lots of information about the area is available. Turn right after the police station as you go along the main street. For more up-market lodgings, there are several motels and rooms at the pub.

Day 14   Port Campbell to Apollo Bay
(100 km/62 miles)

Of all the rides in this book, today's has to be one of the most spectacular—and one of the toughest. You'll see some of the world's most breathtaking coastal scenery in the morning, temperate rain forest at lunch, rugged ranges and beautiful beaches in the afternoon.

Once out of Port Campbell, it's not long before you're at the first formation of the day, Loch Ard Gorge. The clipper ship *Loch Ard* sank off nearby Mutton Bird Island in 1878, and the only two survivors of the tragedy, a man and a woman, were washed ashore at Loch Ard Gorge, where they sheltered overnight in the caves. There are also a couple of other sights well worth visiting here including the Blowholes, Thundercave, and Broken Head. About 12 km into the ride is the most famous of all the sights along this coast, the Twelve

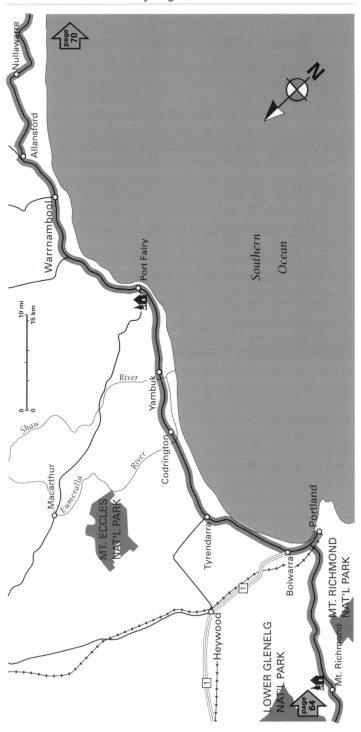

Apostles. Arriving fairly early will probably spare you from hordes of coach parties, allowing you to fully enjoy this wonderful sight, the exquisite result of ravishing erosion over countless centuries.

Not long after the Apostles, the road swings away from the coast, passing through Princetown. The countryside seems to change after the town, becoming decidedly hillier, with several climbs. Eventually a long, exhilarating descent brings you down into a little wooded valley at about the 35 km point. I remember experiencing feelings of sympathy for another cyclist slowly trudging up this hill as my companion and I swooped past in the opposite direction. She must have been quietly grinning to herself in the knowledge that we had almost 20 km of climbing ahead of us.

The road snakes around, up and up, only a few minor descents giving temporary relief to aching legs. Pleasant wooded scenery and some nice views offer momentary distractions during your lengthy ascent into the Otway ranges. Try to settle into a nice rhythm and stay seated whenever possible. At about 52 km, there's a nondescript turnoff to the right leading into Melba Gully State Park.

Although the desire to continue on and reach the top may be strong, I encourage you to take a break here. The park contains a magnificent 65-hectare patch of temperate rain forest, which can be explored on foot by way of a couple of well-constructed walking trails. Be careful on the rocky and steep descent down to the picnic area. From the turnoff to Melba Gully it's only another couple of km to the top of the longest climb in the whole book, and the little settlement of Laver's Hill. There's a good roadhouse with some campground-style accommodation, and a general store about 200 m up the road. The road veers to the right, opposite this general store. Cycle on with the knowledge that you're at the highest point on the Great Ocean Road.

It's time for a reward for all your morning's efforts. The reward comes in the form of a descent close to 20 km long, interrupted only occasionally by a few short climbs, culminating in a white-knuckle descent down to the coast at Glenaire. Head inland again along a flat, fertile valley floor surrounded by lush grassy hills. After a few km, just after the Hordern Vale turnoff, the road begins to rise again. The climb is unrelenting as you snake your way up into the Otway National Park. Although nowhere near as long as the Laver's Hill climb, it's a tough one. Spur yourself on by reminding

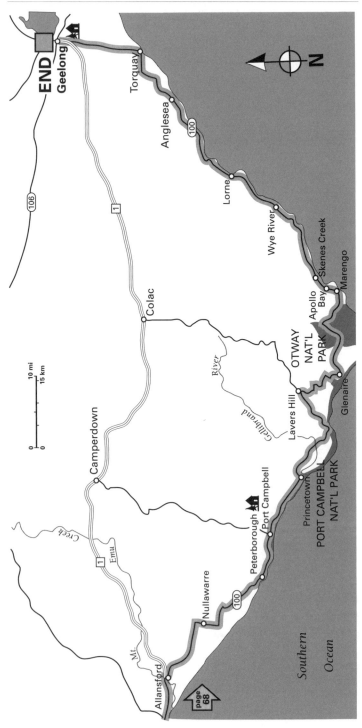

yourself it's the last climb of the day. Magnificent stands of tall timber line the road, a reminder of the past when the Otways once boasted the tallest hardwood forests in the world. Continue ahead past the turnoff to Cape Otway on the right, eventually coming to the entrance to Mait's Rest, another beautiful patch of rain forest with raised boardwalks. About 15 km short of Apollo Bay, you descend again toward the coast, returning to sea level about a km or two before the town.

Once described by Rudyard Kipling as paradise, Apollo Bay lies nestled between Bass Strait and the foot of the Otway ranges. It's a fair-size place, with plenty of shops and recreational facilities. Accommodation is available in the form of many motels, several caravan parks and camping grounds, and an associate YHA hostel. The hostel is situated within the grounds of the Pisces caravan park, which is located on the left side of the road, about a km beyond the town itself. If everywhere is full, try Skene's Creek camping area, by the beach, about 6 km out of town.

Day 15   Apollo Bay to Anglesea
(76 km/47 miles)

The character of the Great Ocean Road changes once again as it leaves Apollo Bay in the direction of Lorne. The narrow, winding road clings to the edges of cliffs high above white beaches and pounding surf. Cape Patton lookout provides great views out over Bass Strait. The road is predominantly flat, with a few small climbs, snaking its way along the coast, passing through the small settlements of Kennett River and Wye River, before bringing you to Lorne at about the 45 km mark. Located on beautiful blue Louttit Bay, Lorne is one of Victoria's oldest and best-loved resort towns, a playground of the well-to-do. An extensive range of up-market and budget accommodation is available, including a backpacker's.

After Lorne, the road rises and falls somewhat, and there seems to be a noticeable increase in the amount of traffic. There is a photo opportunity at about the 58 km point, where an archway emblazoned with the magic words "Great Ocean Road" spans the road. You reach Anglesea after 74 km of rewarding cycling. The town is a spread-out sort of a place, offering a variety of motel and campground accommodation.

Day 16   **Anglesea to Geelong**
half day (39 km/24 miles)

After climbing out of Anglesea and away from the coast, the road levels out, and a bike path provides welcome relief from fairly heavy traffic, especially during weekends and holidays. The path continues more or less all the way to Torquay, 16 km away. Short of the town is the turnoff to Bells Beach, one of Australia's most famous, and host to a round of the world surfing tour. Ignoring an alternative route to Geelong on the left, follow the Great Ocean Road its remaining distance into Torquay, where you turn left at a roundabout and join the Surf Coast Highway for the rest of the journey into Geelong. Torquay is Australia's surf capital, with many leading board and clothing manufacturers headquartered here. There's even Australia's only surfing hall of fame and museum. The bike path takes you most of the way into Geelong, a journey of approximately 23 km.

Geelong is one of Victoria's most historically significant cities, and its second biggest. Situated on Corio Bay, Geelong is well worth exploring. Visit the art gallery, the National Wool Museum, or one of the many other attractions this city has to offer. A wide range of accommodation is available including a YHA hostel, on Lonsdale St.

From Geelong, I advise you to hop on a train for a one-hour trip to the center of Melbourne, avoiding the busy and treacherous roads into the city. To get to Geelong's train station, continue along the highway, eventually climbing a bit of a hill. Turn right at the traffic lights after the hill onto Gordon Ave., where the station is located.

Melbourne

Melbourne comes across as solid, sedate, leafy, and intellectual. It is also a city of great cultural diversity, with some excellent restaurants and lively nightlife areas. Lygon St. in Carlton and Brunswick St. in Fitzroy are particularly popular, with interesting pubs, cafes, and restaurants, and a nice cosmopolitan feel. There are lots of things to do and see.

There is a good choice of places to stay, with two YHA hostels and other budget accommodation both in the city and the seaside suburb of St. Kilda. The YHA hostel Queensberry Hill, on Howard St. in North Melbourne, not far from the Queen Victoria Market is housed in a large refurbished building and is more like a hotel than a hostel.

Chapter 8.
Melbourne to Canberra

This is a tour that really highlights the benefits of going by bike, as you travel through some magnificent wilderness areas rarely seen by car travelers. From Melbourne, you head east through Gippsland and the Latrobe Valley, passing through pleasant farming country and native forests, with easy cycling on quiet roads and the occasional stint on the Princes Highway.

From Bairnsdale you head north to Buchan, home to some magnificent caves, starting your climb into the Australian high country. Beyond Buchan, you enter a large wilderness area dominated by the pristine, alpine beauty of the Snowy River and Kosciusko National Parks. Much of the cycling here is on unsealed

An alpine hut offers emergency shelter atop Australia's highest peak, Mt. Kosciusko.

roads, which slows your pace but restricts motor vehicle access, allowing you to better enjoy your natural surroundings. There are some tough climbs, but they are rewarded with spectacular views and exhilarating descents. You emerge from the wilderness at Jindabyne, a good base for exploring the surrounding mountains, including Australia's highest peak, Mt. Kosciusko.

Continuing north, you pass through drier cattle country to Adaminaby (home of the" Big Trout"), before another wilderness section brings you to the outskirts of Canberra, Australia's capital and home to many monuments and museums worthy of a few days of exploration.

Start	Melbourne (Belgrave train station)
Finish	Canberra
Distance	787 km (488 miles)
Duration	2 weeks (10 cycling days)
Terrain	From Melbourne, through Gippsland as far as Bairnsdale, the terrain is relatively flat, passing predominantly through farming land. After Bairnsdale, however, you encounter considerably more hills, climbing up into the Australian high country and the Snowy Mountains. The terrain is rugged but spectacular, with much of the cycling through national parks on unsealed roads. From Jindabyne to Canberra, there are still a number of significant climbs to tackle, but the landscape is far more open, passing mainly through cattle grazing land.
Road Conditions	The vast bulk of the tour is ridden on quiet country roads with only occasional short stints on the busy Princes Highway. A considerable portion of this tour however is ridden on unsealed roads, most of them in good condition, with long unsealed sections between Buchan and Jindabyne and Adaminaby and Canberra.
Accomm.	It is highly recommended that you carry camping equipment for this tour because of the large wilderness area between Buchan and Jindabyne. It is still possible to ride the tour

without it, but only with advance planning in the form of a booking at the Eagle's Loft B&B at Suggan Buggan, followed by a lengthy, tough ride the following day.

Day 1   ***Melbourne (train to Belgrave) to Warragul***
(80 km/50 miles)

The best way to avoid Melbourne's sprawling suburbs and get straight into some interesting cycling country is to catch one of the commuter trains from Flinders St. station to Belgrave. Belgrave, nestled in the Dandenong ranges, is also the departure point for the famous Puffing Billy railway. The historic narrow-gauge steam train now plies a daily scenic 14 km route to Emerald Lake Park.

From Belgrave, follow the road signed to Emerald and Gembrook. Having gained quite a bit of altitude on the trip to Belgrave, there's only a slight incline to negotiate on your way to Emerald as you travel through some beautiful little valleys dotted with lush tree ferns and tall timber. The road runs beside the Puffing Billy tracks at several points, and if you're fortunate you may catch a glimpse of him along the way. Anyone familiar with Australian TV may recognize the town of Emerald, as the series "A Country Practice" used to be filmed here. Consequently many of the local shops have the words "Wandon Valley" somewhere in their name, a reference to the fictional town in the show rather than any geographical reality. Continue directly ahead through the town toward Cockatoo. Descending a hill coming into Cockatoo, turn left onto another road, signed to Gembrook. Although the route rises and falls somewhat, overall you climb gradually through pleasant farmland and forest to the little town, which lies at about the 28 km point of your ride. There's not much to Gembrook apart from a pub and a general store, both of which offer an opportunity to quench your thirst before continuing.

Turn right onto the road by a pub called the Ranges Hotel, passing Gembrook Park and coming to the Pakenham road, where you once again turn right. After cycling a couple of km, the bitumen road veers right, but you continue straight ahead on the unsealed Bessy Creek Rd. toward Nar Nar Goon. The surface is pretty good as the road descends through some fantasticly lush, wooded scenery, but it deteriorates slightly farther on, due to corrugations. With a

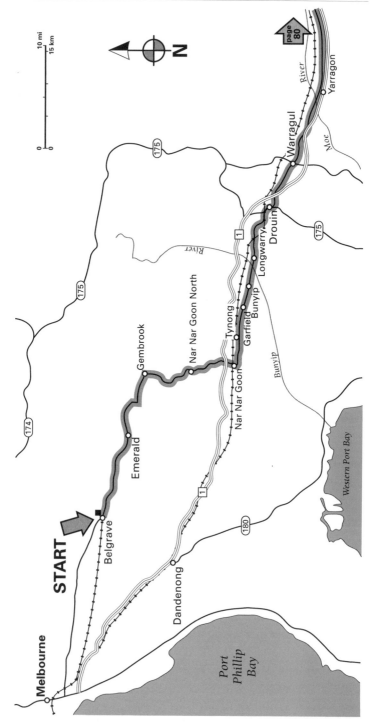

keen eye, though, it's not that difficult to pick out a relatively smooth path through the rough stuff. Sealed road, at the 38 km point, will probably be a welcome sight to you at Nar Nar Goon North, where you continue ahead through fairly flat farming country for several km before reaching the busy Princes Highway.

Cross the highway carefully, and cycle a short distance into the curiously named town of Nar Nar Goon. Take the first left after the railway tracks, signed to Longwarry, onto the road that used to be the Princes Highway before the new one was constructed. The road is flat, straight, and not particularly interesting, but it offers a direct and relatively traffic-free alternative to the main road. Pass through Tynong, Garfield, and Bunyip before reaching Longwarry, where you cross the railway tracks and continue on the road to Drouin. There's a few long, straight climbs to challenge the legs and the mind between Longwarry and Drouin, where you join the busier Warragul bypass. Turning right, you travel through the commercial center of Drouin before reaching the outskirts of Warragul a short distance later.

Warragul is a regional center for the surrounding district's dairy industry, which supplies the bulk of Melbourne's milk. It's a fair -ized place and as such offers a number of accommodation options. At the cheaper end of the spectrum, the Warragul caravan park on Burke St. is quite nice, and offers tent sites and cabins. You'll see the signs for it as you come down a hill into town. There is also some pub- and motel-style accommodation available in town. The Club Hotel in Queens St. is worth a try for a reasonably priced bed.

Day 2   Warragul to Traralgon
(71 km/44 miles)

This day's ride travels through the Latrobe Valley, an area probably known best for its huge deposits of brown coal and the power stations that consume it. Fortunately, heavy industry occupies only a small portion of the valley, which on the whole is a pleasant and fertile place.

Find your way out of Warragul and out on to the Princes Freeway (bikes permitted), heading in the direction of Moe. Although the traffic is pretty much what you would expect of a major road, the very wide shoulder makes cycling along it a tolerable experience. After 15 km of easy cycling, you arrive in Yarragon, where you leave the highway behind. Cross the

railway line to head down Shady Creek Rd. for a few km
before taking a little-used road off to the right, just after
crossing a small bridge over the Moe River (18.8 km). The
road looks as if it was sealed once upon a time, but now it's
fairly rough in places. In contrast to the first part of today's
ride, however, you're virtually assured a traffic-free
experience. Cycling along with nothing but the sound of your
jingling panniers to disturb you, you come to appreciate the
fact that although the highway offers a fast, direct, and often
tempting route between destinations, the real joy of cycle
touring can best be experienced along these back roads where
it's just you, your bike, and Mother Nature.

With the Moe River off to your right and dairy pasture to
your left, the lane comes to an end at approximately the
31 km mark, a "no through road" sign blocking your path.
Take the road leading uphill off to the left for a short distance
before turning right onto another predominantly unsealed
way known as Millers Rd. After a while, Millers Rd. joins a
busier, sealed route that leads you down into the town of
Moe, visible at this stage, down to your right. Moe, a coal
mining center, is one of the main towns of the Latrobe Valley
and as such has most of the facilities you would expect.

Leave town by heading east along the main road, coming
to a set of traffic lights where you continue ahead and to the
left toward Yallourn. The route can be a bit confusing, but the
sight of the large cooling towers of the Yallourn "W" Power
Station is a sign that you're on the right track. Just in front of
the power station, the road forks and branches in several
different directions. Keep to the left, heading toward Yallourn
North. The route becomes a little hillier as you start to reach
the far edge of the valley, continuing past Yallourn North and
on to the small settlement of Tyers. The roadhouse, with the
opportunity to purchase an icy cold drink, was a welcome
sight on the day I passed through, as the weather was
oppressively hot and humid. Begin the last leg of the day's
ride by heading out of town, turning right onto a road signed
to Traralgon, by a roadside rest area a few km out of Tyers.
Stay on this road for the remainder of your journey into town.

Traralgon is the center of Victoria's paper and pulp
industry and is also a major electricity producer, the massive
Loy Yang power station lying 6 km south of town.
Accommodation is available at the Park Lane caravan park,
and at several pubs and motels. Lyons hotel, a big old place, is
comfortable and very well priced. The Princes Highway runs

through town, so the major fast food outlets are well represented. The people at Pizza Hut didn't know what hit them when my companion and I set about exploiting their all-you-can-eat deal. They're probably trying to figure out a way to ban ravenous cyclists in the future. Also opposite the highway are the botanical gardens, which provide a great place to stretch out under the trees at the end of the day and watch the sun go down.

Day 3   Traralgon to Valencia Creek
(90 km/56 miles)

Facilities at Valencia Creek are limited to a fairly basic, isolated caravan park, although some on-site vans are available. As an alternative you could make your way on slightly busier roads to the larger center of Maffra, where there are more extensive accommodation options and facilities, rejoining the main ride at Valencia Creek the next day. If you wish to do this, leave the route described below at Heyfield.

To leave Traralgon, find your way onto the Princes Highway and head in the direction of Sale, which probably means turning left. Cycle up the highway for a couple of km, passing through a predominantly light industrial area, before taking another left onto a road signed to Heyfield. Farmland doesn't make for the most exciting scenery, but the terrain is flat and the road generally straight, making for fairly easy cycling as you pass by Glengarry (9 km) before coming to Toongabbie (19 km). Turn left by the general store and head up a narrow but sealed country lane, devoid of traffic, toward Cowarr Weir. After a while you come to an intersection where you have a choice of continuing straight ahead to the Weir or turning right toward Cowarr itself. Although the road to the Weir is a dead end, requiring backtracking, it's not very far and is a pleasant place to have a bit of a rest. The Weir itself (27 km) is surrounded by some nice shady grassed areas with picnic and toilet facilities.

Back out on the road, head toward Cowarr, turning left toward Seaton and Dawson just before you reach the town itself. Pass through one intersection before coming to another a short distance later, where you make a right turn onto Dawson Rd., signed to Dawson and Heyfield. Heyfield is a quiet country town, but it has a few shops on its main street, including a supermarket, making it a good destination for lunch. Leave town via Weir Rd., which may be a little bit

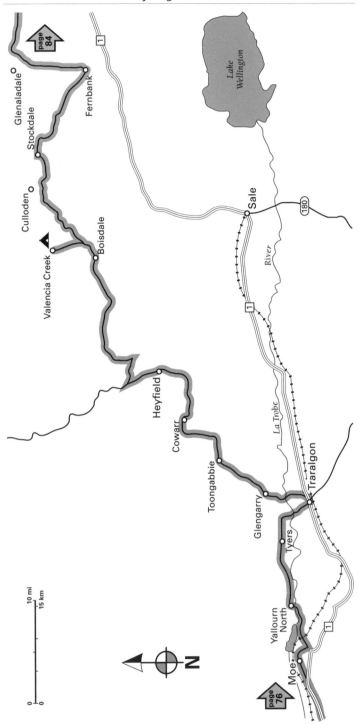

tricky to find. Here are basic directions. Follow the main street around, turning right by a milk bar. Weir Rd. is on the left, a large tree marking the corner. If in doubt, ask a local.

Follow Weir Rd., eventually coming to an intersection where you follow the signs for the Weir Wall (a quick right then left). The road is surrounded by dense bushland on both sides, making the sighting of a kangaroo a distinct possibility. At about the 56 km point, you cross a small bridge known as Lannigan's bridge, before coming to an intersection a short distance later, where you turn right signed to Newry (10 km). Straight ahead is a no-through road leading to Lake Glenmaggie, a water catchment area that is also a popular spot for fishing and boating. A few km later, you pass through the small village of Upper Maffra West. Take a left turn a short distance on toward Boisdale, eventually joining a larger road where you turn left once more. You reach the Boisdale intersection at about the 75 km point, left to Valencia Creek, right to Boisdale. You might want to make a quick detour into town to buy some supplies, as there is no food available at the campground. Head out toward Valencia Creek, which the sign misleadingly tells you is only 6 km away. The few scattered houses that comprise the village appear about 9 km later, the campground being some way farther on. Turn left at a crossroads just beyond the village, eventually turning left again by a sawmill, signed to the caravan park. Traveling along this road, you begin to wonder if there's ever going to be a caravan park, a quick scan of the countryside revealing no likely locations. After a couple of km however, a sign over the road signals your arrival. Pay at the farmhouse by the entrance and make your way down a rutted track (dodging cows), to the rather primitive camping area. Fortunately the showers are in good working order and feel like heaven at the end of a rather long day in the saddle.

Day 4   *Valencia Creek to Bairnsdale*
(85 km/53 miles)

Retrace your steps a little from yesterday, heading back up to the sawmill and turning right. After cycling for about 6 km, you come to a crossroads, where you should head left in the direction of Briagolong. The terrain is fairly flat and the roads nearly deserted as you pedal along in the cool morning air. Not long after crossing the Freestone Creek bridge, you come to another crossroads at the 14 km point. You should continue straight ahead here following the sealed road signed to Stockdale. The quiet, narrow road is quickly enveloped by dense state forest, making for a beautiful cycling environment. Arriving early in the morning makes an encounter with a kangaroo here a distinct likelihood. Riding along, you'll notice a red marker sign on the side of the road signaling the route of the Howitt bicycle trail. Take note of it as you'll be following it for almost the rest of the day.

The Howitt trail comprises several shortish rides around the Gippsland area, marked by the distinctive red signs you've just seen. If you're interested in exploring the Gippsland area by bike, the Howitt trail offers a good way to do it. Information about the rides is available in the form of a booklet, sold at local tourist information centers (available in Bairnsdale) at a modest price. After 22 km you arrive at a T-junction, where you turn left, following the Howitt trail.

Passing through a pleasant mix of pine plantations and farmland, veer left at a fork in the road at the 28 km point, signed to Fernbank. The pleasant, traffic-free cycling continues, lush pockets of greenery, dense with ferns, signaling that the town can't be too distant. After 41 km you arrive at an intersection with Fernbank just off to your right. It's a quiet little place with no shops or services, but it serves as a nice enough spot to take a break. While my friend and I were sitting on the grass in front of the church having lunch, a flock of hundreds of sheep came wandering up the road, making for an unusual sight. It was only after quite a while that the farmer at the rear of the flock in his 4WD became visible. Anyway, turn left at the Fernbank intersection, continuing to follow the Howitt trail signed to Dargo. After approximately 50 km, and not long after passing by a communications tower, the route comes to a crossroads, where you continue straight ahead. After a few km, the route descends to a valley floor, the enjoyable downhill bringing a change in the scenery. Pass over the Iguana Creek bridge and sweep along the valley floor through a mixture of farmland and fertile market gardens. With little wind, it's easy to sustain a cracking pace along this flat stretch of road, coming to the Wuk Wuk bridge after 65 km.

Not far up the road at another crossroads, take a left, continuing to follow the Howitt trail signed toward Bairnsdale, coming to the town of Lindenow a short while later. Unlike most of the places so far today, Lindenow does have some shops and even a pub, where it is possible to indulge in some well-earned refreshment. Not far out of town, the road veers to the right, the Howitt trail carrying on straight ahead. It's possible to follow the trail, but it's probably just as well to stay on the road, as the trail joins it again shortly anyway. Traffic along this stretch increases slightly, but it's still not too bad. This is scenically not all that inspiring, but it remains flat, making for some pretty easy cycling. You eventually come out onto the busy Princes Highway at the 81 km point, turning left to head into the major town of Bairnsdale lying only a short distance away.

Bairnsdale (pop. 11,500), situated on the Mitchell River, is the administrative and commercial hub of east Gippsland. Blessed with plenty of facilities, nice gardens, and a wide main street, it still manages to retain a relaxed country feel. The town serves as a popular base for people exploring the attractions of the surrounding area, which include the mountains to the north and the lakes to the south. Arriving in Bairnsdale, I was pleasantly surprised to find a great backpacker hostel not listed in my guide book. Bairnsdale Backpackers at 119 Macleod St. is located near the middle of town, right next to the train station. It's a small place but very friendly and a good value. Motels, pubs, and caravan parks are also well represented. For those of you in a hurry to get to or from Melbourne, Bairnsdale lies on the main rail line, with daily services to Victoria's capital. It's also served by all of the major bus companies plying the coastal route between Melbourne and Sydney.

Day 5   Bairnsdale to Buchan
(77 km/48 miles)

Today's ride leaves the relatively flat terrain encountered so far and heads for the hills, going into some fairly tough but beautiful country, to the town of Buchan, a gateway to the famous Snowy River wilderness area.

A couple of km out of Bairnsdale, the Princes Highway forks. Take the left fork, the Omeo Highway signed to Bruthen, Buchan, and Omeo. It's not long before you start to climb up some moderately long and steep inclines, the tolerably busy road rising more than falling on its way to Bruthen at the 25 km point. The town has a nice grassed area along its main street, providing a good place to recuperate from the first of the day's efforts. Leave the Omeo Highway

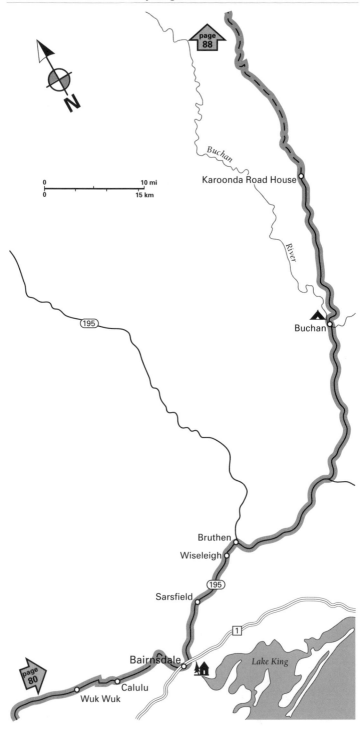

in Bruthen, heading instead toward your final destination for the day, Buchan.

Beyond Bruthen, the road continues to rise, passing through dense state forest on both sides, making for tiring but enjoyable cycling. The road forks at the 48 km mark, where you head left signed to Buchan and perhaps more tantalizingly Jindabyne (199 km), your destination (after some tough riding) in a couple of days' time. Just near the fork in the road, there's a well-constructed three-sided shelter, marked by a Howitt trail marker, offering good protection from the elements if required. The rest of the route to Buchan, like that so far, is through fantastic forest and bush, the rolling road interspersed with a couple of longish, tough climbs. As a reward, the final couple of km into town are all downhill, providing an exhilarating finish to the day's ride, arriving in town after approximately 77 km.

Buchan lies at the gateway to the Snowy River wilderness, and serves as base to tour operators offering whitewater rafting and horse riding adventures. The chief attraction of the town itself is its caves, which are open daily for guided tours. Conveniently, the camping area, operated by the National Parks Service, lies within the reserve that houses the caves, providing shady, grassed camping sites and good toilet facilities. While camping, be sure to keep your food tucked away, as many kangaroos roam the reserve after dark looking for a meal. The town also has a motel and some cabin-style lodgings in the area.

Make sure to stock up on supplies in Buchan, as the next real town, Jindabyne, is at least two days' ride away, with no real accommodation apart from camping in between.

Day 6 *Buchan to Suggan Buggan*
(83 km/51 miles)

Today's ride takes you away from civilization and into the heart of the Snowy River wilderness area, skirting the Snowy River National Park. The countryside is spectacular and virtually traffic-free, ensuring some terrific cycling, which, although tough at times, is ultimately a rewarding experience.

Making you pay for yesterday's descent into town, the road begins to climb in a gradual but continuous fashion almost immediately, leaving little time for you to shake off any early morning lethargy. The assent continues through the increasingly scenic countryside for about 7 km before leveling and eventually plunging to the valley floor, by way of a long, winding downhill at around the 14 km point. Having lost much of the altitude gained, it's not long before you start to climb again. Prepare yourself for some hard work, as apart from the natural beauty of your surroundings, there's little relief from climbing for quite a while. A waterfall at the 21 km point called W-Tree Falls provides an enticing opportunity to pull off the road, have a drink and a bite to eat, and give your legs a well-earned rest.

The road, flanked by attractive bushland and the occasional grazing property, continues its journey skyward, taking you into the legendary Australian high country. The going gets tougher around the 35 km mark, as the road becomes unsealed near Butcher's Ridge. The unsealed surface is generally in fairly good condition, although this will fluctuate somewhat according to such factors as recent weather, traffic, and the time since last graded. Arriving at Gelantipy after 42 km, you might wonder how on earth you're going to make it to Suggan Buggan, but let me assure you that the first half of the day is definitely the hardest—much of the remaining distance is either flat or downhill (the last 10 km in fact). Gelantipy, although probably marked on your map, really consists of nothing more than the Karoonda Road House, which also operates as a camp conducting horse riding holidays. The small store provides an opportunity to

North of Buchan, the terrain becomes decidedly hillier.

purchase a cold drink and is also the last reliable source of supplies before Jindabyne.

Just beyond Gelantipy the road becomes sealed again, but unfortunately, the comparative luxury the smooth surface offers is short lived, petering out after a km or two. The route is relatively flat in comparison to the morning's ride, however, and makes an enjoyable and rare descent down to the valley floor at Boundary Creek at the 56 km mark. A few km down the road is the Seldom Seen roadhouse, offering little but the chance to purchase last- minute provisions. According to local reports, its operating hours are sporadic to say the least. The road continues to rise and fall as it winds its way through the traffic-free wilderness. A vigilant eye is required on descents in order to avoid ruts and deep pockets of gravel that can easily result in a painful tumble. On the left side of the road at the 72 km point lies the Eagles Loft Gallery B&B. This is the only fixed accommodation in the area. A stay here and a very tough ride to Jindabyne the following day is the only possible way to avoid having to camp. Make sure to book ahead if this is your plan.

A short distance up the road from the B&B, you round a bend and begin to descend. It is only now that you can really appreciate just how far you have climbed during the day, a quick look out across the valley indicating that you really are a long way up. Now the fun really starts, as there's no need to touch the pedals for virtually the rest of the day—10 km all downhill. The temptation to not touch the brakes is strong, but nevertheless a cautious descent is advised on the slippery and corrugated surface.

Relieved and exhilarated, pull into the campsite at Suggan Buggan and congratulate yourself on a hard day's work well done. The campsite is pleasantly situated next to the Suggan Buggan River, which by all reports is safe to drink, although boiling first may be a wise precaution, especially in summer. The only facility at the site is a dry toilet, although the river provides a refreshing but chilly means of splashing away the day's dirt and grime. Once you've set up camp, you might want to wander over and take a look at the original schoolhouse that still stands nearby as a solitary reminder of times gone by.

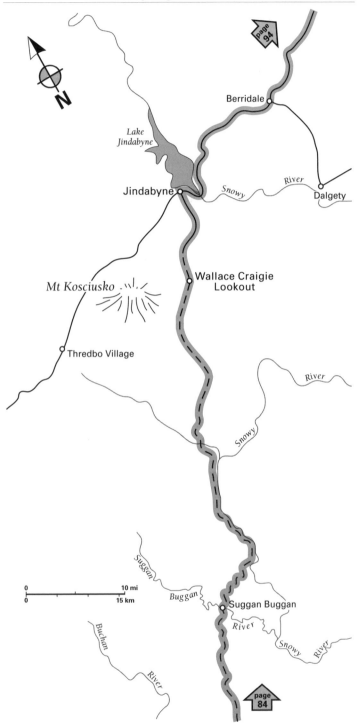

Day 7   ***Suggan Buggan to Jindabyne***
(95 km/59 miles)

This difficult but memorable day may be broken into two by overnighting at one of the several campsites on the route nestled alongside the magnificent Snowy River.

Leaving Suggan Buggan, it's not long before you start making up altitude lost on yesterday's long descent, although I'm happy to say that the climb out is nowhere near as long. I extend my sympathies to you if you're doing this tour in reverse. As you zigzag up the side of the hill, the valley floor quickly drops away, the initial fairly steep climb lasting approximately 4 km. Once you reach the top, the route rises and falls for a while before an unexpected descent brings you down to the banks of the Snowy river at the 13 km point.

The Snowy river is one of Australia's more famous waterways, primarily (apart from its natural beauty) because of "The Man from Snowy River," a poem by Banjo Patterson, that immortalizes the exploits of the region's horse riding mountain cattle men and has entrenched itself as a part of Australian folklore. Despite the name, the river is surprisingly warm to bathe in during summer, as its shallow, broad path effectively soaks up the sun's rays. I remember a friend of mine saying that in addition to perhaps more obvious exploits such as climbing Ayres Rock, a swim in the Snowy was one of the "must do" experiences in Australia. If the weather is favorable I'd certainly recommend it as a refreshing method of washing off some of the trail dust that has no doubt accumulated about your person.

After 20 km, bid farewell to the state of Victoria and the Alpine National Park, as you cross over into New South Wales (NSW) and the Kosciusko National Park, at Willis (just a sign by the road). Kosciusko National Park not only contains Australia's highest peak, Mt. Kosciusko (2,228 m), but also NSW's largest national park, encompassing some 6,900 sq. km. At the border crossing, there is a camping area with toilets and tables, pleasantly situated next to the Snowy river. This is the first of several such camping areas in the space of 10 km or so. The road remains fairly flat as you continue to follow the river, although the corrugated surface prevents the going from becoming too easy. A bonus of the rocky road that you can't overlook is that while it is tolerable for the intrepid cycle tourer, it's rough enough to deter most vacationing motorists, thus making travel through this beautiful wilderness area that much more pleasurable. After the Running Waters campsite at the 31 km mark, a short, steep climb brings you to Jack's Point lookout, where the viewing platform offers some fine elevated views out across the Snowy.

Finally, after 41 km, you come to the Jacob's River campsite turnoff, a short descent down an access trail bringing you to the river and the camping area itself. This is the last established camping site before Jindabyne, so if you're planning to do Suggan Buggan to Jindabyne in two days, this is probably a good place to stop. That was my original intention, but arriving shortly after lunch, I decided it was too early to call it a day and decided to press on. There's some serious climbing from this point on, so if you have the time and enough food and so on, relax, take a break, and tackle the climb with fresh legs in the morning. For those of you eager to get to Jindabyne and a soft bed, make sure you stock up with water, as Jacob's river is the last good source.

Not long after you leave Jacob's river, the climbing begins. It's more or less relentless for the next 10 km or so, the fine views offering some compensation for weary legs screaming out for a rest. Across the valley you can see where your route eventually leads, but progress up the constantly rising road can be frustratingly slow. I was tempted to rest often, but rationed myself to drink stops every 15 minutes, aware of the need to stay hydrated with such exertion. At the 54 km point, you reach a summit at the Wallace Craigie lookout. Take a well-earned rest, and soak in the panorama. The road up which you've just traveled is clearly visible far below on the opposite side of the valley. Incredulous motorists also admiring the view will undoubtedly quiz you on your cycling travel plans, amazed by your stamina in conquering the hill.

Despite some wishful thinking, it's not all downhill from the Wallace Craigie lookout to Jindabyne. In fact, there's still a fair bit of climbing ahead. The scenery begins to change as the pristine wilderness is replaced by high-country grazing pastures, and the road becomes sandier. Large yellow flies capable of inflicting a harmless but painful bite seem to abound in the area, making rest stops less pleasurable than they ought to be. Probably much to your relief, at the 68 km point the unsealed road that has been your companion almost from Buchan becomes sealed again, and the route flattens out somewhat. The sensation of being back on bitumen after such a long time is incredible, as it seems to require hardly any effort to sustain a cracking pace. Revitalized by the alien sensation of speed and a silky smooth ride, the remaining 27 km to Jindabyne pass fairly quickly, although there are several annoying climbs to negotiate, including a testing rise about 6 km out of town. This represents your final obstacle to relaxation; you cruise the final km downhill to Lake Jindabyne, and a right turn at the roundabout brings you to the town.

Jindabyne is situated on the shores of the artificial Lake Jindabyne, created as part of the Snowy Mountains Hydroelectric Scheme. It's a modern town dominated by the tourist industry, which during the ski season (July–September) swells the modest population considerably. Activities in summer revolve around the lake. Windsurfing boards and and other water craft can be hired, and many anglers fish for the elusive trout that inhabit the lake.

Accommodation options include two caravan parks and numerous motels and ski lodges, which discount their prices considerably during summer (or should I say massively inflate their prices during winter), although for the budget-minded cyclist they may still be a little on the expensive side. The best budget option is a fantastic place called Lazy Harry's (where I stayed). It's a ski lodge situated right next to the lake as you cycle into town, offering cheap beds in a very comfortable and clean setting. It's not really a backpacker place but has similarly priced rooms and offers a 10% discount to YHA members. It's one of the best budget accommodation places I've come across in my cycling travels. For a meal, the Bowling Club serves an all-you-can- eat salad bar affair.

Day 8   *Jindabyne to Adaminaby*
(88 km/55 miles)

Today's ride takes you away from the ski fields and through cattle grazing country, to Berridale and Adaminaby, home of the "Big Trout." There's some climbing in the early parts of the ride, flattening out to rolling hills the rest of the way. It's hard to imagine that it snows in these parts, as it can get very hot, the parched brown landscape testimony to the intensity of the summer sun. Carry plenty of water—there aren't many places to refill along the way.

Leave Jindabyne in the direction of Berridale, passing over the dam wall a short distance out of town. As you skirt the lake, you begin to climb and continue to do so for several km, eventually passing through East Jindabyne. After 12 km or so, the route flattens out considerably, although it continues to rise and fall. The wilderness surroundings of the last few days are replaced by grazing pastures, which in summer appear brown and parched. Traffic is not too bad but is generally fast-moving. You reach a summit after 22 km at Varney's Range, a sign on the roadside indicating an altitude of 1,080 m, a gain of some 160 vertical meters from Jindabyne. The rest of the distance into Berridale is more or less a very slight downhill. The town is fairly small but has a few shops where you can buy a cold drink, food, and so on. There is also a motel, but there are really not many reasons to stay here.

Pressing on, take the Adaminaby road out of Berridale. This road is considerably quieter than the Alpine Way, but unfortunately seems to have a constant gradual uphill inclination. The brown grazing land continues, and although not particularly visually stimulating, imparts a feeling of wide open space. My strongest memory of this section of the ride is of thousands of little grasshoppers, flying out of the grass by the sides of the road, startled by the sound of my passing bike. Eventually the gradual uphill seems to give way to a frustrating series of ups and downs. After working hard to climb a hill, the enjoyment of the trip down the other side is cut short by the immediate appearance of another. These hills aren't particularly large, but they can be annoying after a while.

You reach another summit at the 63 km point when you reach the Snowy/Murrumbidgee Divide at an elevation of 1,317 m. This point marks the division between the catchment areas for the Snowy and Murrumbidgee Rivers. From this point on, the going gets considerably easier. A short distance on, you join the Snowy Mountains Highway, turning left in the direction of Adaminaby. The last 15 km or so into town are pretty much downhill or flat, making for some good speeds and a relatively easy end to the day.

Adaminaby is most famous for its trout fishing in nearby Lake Eucumbene. As a testament to the local sportfishing industry, the "Big Trout," a large, hideous concrete statue, stands proudly in the middle of town. Adaminaby has a couple of motels, a caravan park, and a pub offering basic but cheap accommodation. Look out for the fisherman's special at only $10 for a bed for the night. The pub also serves some good-quality, cheap food.

Day 9   *Adaminaby to Canberra*
(118km/73 miles)

When tackled in one day this is a long and tough ride, but it is by no means impossible. The ride may be spread over two easier days by overnighting at one of a couple of campsites along the route. Much of the ride is on unsealed roads passing through hilly terrain, which take you through some nice traffic-free countryside, though they can also make for tough cycling at times.

Leaving Adaminaby, it is necessary to backtrack on yesterday's ride a little, turning left after a km or two onto a road signed to Canberra (105 km, 45 km gravel road). After 7.5 km you cross a small bridge over the Murrumbidgee River. A short distance later you leave the luxury of sealed road behind, continuing on a fairly rough and in places soft and sandy surface. The road begins to climb and continues to do so for some time. The combination of considerable inclines, a sandy surface, and, in summer, hot and fairly shadeless terrain, makes for some pretty tough going. However, having already negotiated some substantially bigger climbs earlier in the tour (remember Suggan Buggan to Jindabyne), these hills are best described as challenging rather than tortuous.

There's a brief respite from climbing at Shannon's Flat before your upward journey continues as you cross the border into the Australian Capital Territory (ACT) and enter the Namadji National Park. After approximately 36 km of cycling, you reach the turnoff to the Mt. Clear campsite on your right-hand side. This is the first of two campsites, suitable as an overnight stopping point, allowing the journey to Canberra to be made in two easier days. The access trail to the camping area is fairly long (about 2 km) and predominantly downhill, so unless you intend to stay, you may want to consider whether it's worth just taking a break there. The camp site itself consists of a large open grassy area, with a dry toilet, firewood supplied, and Naas Creek down the back. When I visited this site in the middle of summer, the water level in the creek was extremely low and certainly not suitable for drinking. Water taken from here should probably be boiled before consumption.

Back out on the main trail, it's not long before you find yourself at the base of one of the tougher climbs in this book. The first 2 km of this 6 km ascent are definitely the worst, the

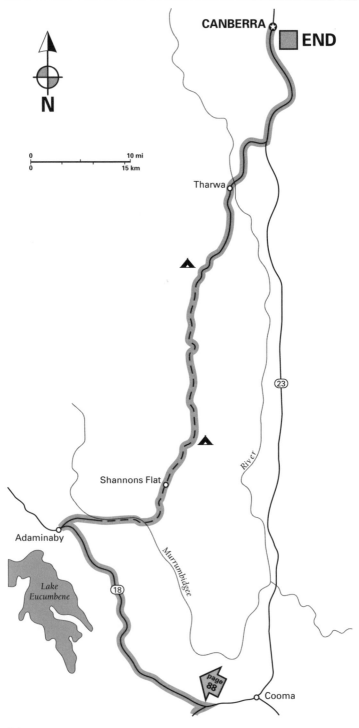

N

0 ————— 10 mi
0 ————— 15 km

CANBERRA

END

Tharwa

Shannons Flat

Adaminaby

Lake
Eucumbene

Murrumbidgee

River

18

23

page
88

Cooma

sheer steepness of the incline and the loose surface making it difficult for the rear wheel of your bike to get traction. Spur yourself on by thinking about the fact that once at the top of this hill, approximately 1,400 m above sea level, you have roughly 900 vertical meters to lose by the time you get to Canberra. Take a break at the top, pat yourself on the back, and prepare yourself for some hair-raising descents. Traveling downhill on the loose, sliding surface presents a bit of dilemma. Do you lay off the brakes, get maximum benefit from all your hard work while risking life and limb, or chew through your brake blocks placing greater importance on your health than on a temporary adrenalin rush. My riding partner for this tour is of the former school of thought while I am of the latter, the instinct of self-preservation overwhelming all others. Although on this section of the tour he broke the magical 80 km/hr barrier (85 km/hr in fact) and lived to tell the tale, eventually he came to grief and had to return home, leaving me solo, after his hang-loose riding style saw him slide halfway down Mt. Ainslie in Canberra. I think there's a lesson in that somewhere. Anyway, much of the danger in such high-speed descents is removed when you rejoin the sealed road at about the 50 km point.

Once on the sealed road, there are a couple of exhilarating downhills interspersed with a few small climbs. At the 60 km mark at Glendale Crossing, on the left-hand side of the road there are a grassed area and a toilet block with running water, providing a welcome opportunity to refill water bottles that have undoubtedly been emptied. Approximately 6 km later, you join another road coming in from the left. The second campground can be reached by traveling down this road, and is located on the right side, shortly after crossing the Ororal River. If heading for Canberra, continue straight ahead.

After a gradual climb of 2 km or so, you reach the top of Fitz's Hill (960 m above sea level). This is an extremely steep incline of some fame, being the subject of an annual bike race from Canberra, up to the top and back again. If you're going to set a speed record, this is where it's going to happen. Keep your adrenalin under control, however, as there are a few turns to negotiate on the way down, making it important that you maintain a manageable speed. Once safely at the bottom, continue along on the sealed road, passing through farming country and bushland, reaching the small town of Tharwa at the 84 km point of the ride. It's a small settlement on the

Murrumbidgee River, but it has a general store where the opportunity to purchase a cold drink will undoubtedly be a welcome one.

Once over the bridge, you reach the outer suburbs of Canberra surprisingly quickly. Unfortunately they seem to be spreading outward at such a rate that by the time you cycle here, I wouldn't be surprised if Tharwa is itself an outer suburb.

Predictably, as you reach the suburbs the traffic increases considerably. Canberra has an extensive system of bicycle paths, but the signs are woefully inadequate, making it extremely difficult for non-locals to know which paths to take. As a guide, pass through Woden and look for a road called Yamba Dr., which turns into Adelaide Ave. and eventually brings you to State Circle and the new Parliament House. If you get lost, which is fairly easy to do, all I can suggest is that you ask a local cyclist for directions to Parliament House, from which it is relatively easy to navigate around Canberra's planned heart.

Day 10   Canberra

At the time of federation in 1901 it was decided that a new national capital should be built, partly to avoid fierce interstate rivalry between Melbourne and Sydney. An international design competition was held, with the eventual winner, American architect Walter Burley Griffin, chosen to have his vision turned into reality. Today, the carefully planned nature of Canberra is easily visible, with key Commonwealth buildings, including the old and new Parliament House, the High Court, the National Library, the War Memorial and the National Gallery, all contained within an area known as Parliamentary Triangle. The city is planned around the body of water bearing the architect's name, Lake Burley Griffin, with most of the buildings mentioned above located on the south side. To the north is the city center, known as Civic, where most of the shops, hotels and office buildings can be found. The Captain Cook Memorial water jet, in the middle of the lake, spews a column of water up to a 140 m in the air, providing the city with a spectacular centerpiece.

Canberra has a reputation of being soulless and dull. As a visitor, however, I can't see why. There are enough national exhibits, museums, and monuments to easily fill a few days' sightseeing. At the top of your list should be a guided tour around the new Parliament House (free), built at a cost of over $1 billion and opened by the Queen in 1988. Also concentrated in the area around the new Parliament House are a number of other attractions, many free of charge, including the old Parliament House, the High Court, the National Library, the National Gallery and Questacon—the National Science and Technology Center—which houses a fantastic collection of hands-on, science-oriented exhibits. Directly opposite Parliament on the other side of the lake, at the end of Anzac Parade, is the National War Memorial, housing the tomb of the unknown soldier and a fine and moving collection of exhibits from the various conflicts to which Australia has been a party. Other attractions worth a look include the National Film and Sound Archives, the Mint and the Australian Institute of Sport. Fine views of Canberra and the surrounding area can be had from the Telecom tower perched on top of Black Mountain.

Getting around Canberra is easy thanks to a good network of bike paths, with everything located within a reasonably compact area. Accommodation options, as you would expect in the nation's capital, are numerous, including hotels, motels, a caravan park, and an excellent YHA hostel. The Canberra YHA hostel lies in the suburb of O'Connor,

An upstream view of the pristine Snowy River near Suggan Buggan.

across Lake Burley Griffin, near the base of Black Mountain. The caravan park is situated almost next door.

To get there from Parliament, cycle across the bridge over the lake, and continue up Northbourne Ave., the main street through Canberra City. Eventually you reach MacArthur Ave., where you turn left. After a km or so take a right into Dryandra St., where you first pass the caravan park and then the YHA hostel, which is set back from the road in a pleasant bushland setting. The lack of many other budget accommodation options ensures that this hostel is always busy, making it advisable to ring ahead in order to avoid disappointment.

Chapter 9.
Canberra to Sydney

This is a fairly short but at times challenging tour from the nation's capital to Australia's biggest city. From Canberra you cycle through the rich wool-growing areas around Goulburn, heading up into a sparsely populated area dominated by the magnificent Blue Mountains National Park. You pass through beautiful Jenolan,

home of the grand and historic caves, before reaching Sydney's sprawling outskirts via the scenic Old Bells Line of Road, making your way safely to the heart of the harbor city by suburban commuter train.

Lush pastures and beautiful valley views in the Blue Mountains between Jenolan and Lithgow.

Start	Canberra
Finish	Sydney (Richmond train station)
Distance	377 km (234 miles)
Duration	7 days (5 cycling days)
Terrain	This route is flat at first, passing predominantly through fertile grazing land, becoming quite hilly, especially near Jenolan, and fairly rugged beyond Goulburn as you head into the Blue Mountains.
Road Conditions	You cycle on the busy Federal Highway on Day 1, although there is a good, wide shoulder most of the way. Much of Days 2 and 3 are on unsealed roads, generally in good condition, with very little traffic. The rest of the route from Jenolan Caves is on sealed roads with light traffic to Lithgow, increasing the closer you get to Richmond, although remaining only moderate.
Accomm.	Advisable to carry camping equipment, as camping is the only option at Abercrombie River, and there are no other budget accommodations at Jenolan Caves. Backpacker accommodation available in Lithgow and Katoomba. There are motels, pubs, and caravan parks in other places along the route.

Day 1   Canberra to Goulburn
(95 km/60 miles)

Today's ride is predominantly along the fairly busy Federal Highway, making for a not particularly exciting but easy day's cycling to Goulburn, an historic town situated in the middle of prime wool-growing country. The width and quality of the shoulder on the highway varies considerably throughout the course of the day, but it is pretty good overall, especially for the second half of the ride. Scenery throughout the day is pleasant enough, consisting mainly of fairly flat farming country. Leaving Canberra is fairly easy; just get on Northbourne Ave. (the main street) and head north out of the city. Before long you reach the Federal Highway, where you turn right to join it. At the time of writing, this first section of highway was not in particularly good shape, having just one lane in either direction and carrying a fair few trucks. Thankfully, I noticed signs of impending road works, so perhaps things have improved a bit. The first few km out of Canberra are slightly uphill, nothing serious but certainly enough to be noticeable.

After about 15 km the road divides and a lane-width shoulder appears, making life far more pleasant. There's a couple of long, gradual uphill stretches to negotiate before you round a bend at the 30 km point and catch your first glimpse of the expansive body of water that is Lake George. The road skirts the lake, making for some fairly fast, flat cycling, with some good views across to hills on the far shore. Several roadside picnic areas along this stretch provide an opportunity to take a break and enjoy the view.

After about 50 km the road becomes divided again, a sign by the road indicating that it remains this way for the next 48 km, the remainder of the distance to Goulburn. Not far from this point is a turnoff on the left to the town of Collector, the only settlement along the route. Unless you're in need of some food there's really no compelling reason to stop here, as unfortunately its glory days appear to be long gone. Having said that, it's only a short detour to the town, and it serves to break the monotony of the highway. A Shell roadhouse sells food and has limited supplies of other goods.

Back out on the highway, the km pass quickly thanks to a flat, smooth surface and a wide shoulder. After 73 km or so you pass a sign by the side of the road that informs you that you are on part of the Great Dividing Range and 740 m above sea level. A little further down the road, the Federal Highway merges with the busier Hume Highway, but fortunately the shoulder remains very wide, keeping cycling conditions tolerable.

Finally, after one of the easier 90 km or so you're likely to encounter, the exit off the highway into Goulburn leads away to the left. After passing the odd assortment of light industrial buildings that generally occupy the outskirts of most towns, you encounter a hideous and typically Australian structure, the "Big Merino." This three-story-high sheep, complete with eyes that glow green at night, stands as a monument to the rich wool industry of the surrounding area. If you're so inclined you can even go inside and see displays and demonstrations showcasing the local wool industry.

From the "Big Merino" there are still a couple of km to the center of town, passing an assortment of motels and a

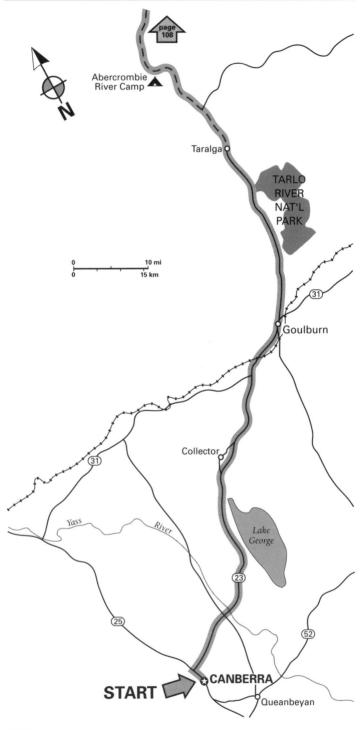

page 108

Abercrombie
River Camp

Taralga

TARLO
RIVER
NAT'L
PARK

0 ——— 10 mi
0 ——— 15 km

(31)

Goulburn

Collector

(31)

Yass *River*

Lake George

(23)

(25)

(52)

START

CANBERRA

Queanbeyan

caravan park on the way. Goulburn, founded in 1833, is quite a large town, with approximately 24,000 inhabitants. There are some fine examples of early architecture about town, including the Riversdale Coaching House built in 1840. The tourist information center, located opposite Belmore Park, has details of a self-paced walking tour around Goulburn, providing a good way to get away from the bike for a couple of hours and see the best of what the town has to offer. They also have a guide to the available accommodation, which unfortunately at the time of writing does not include any backpacker establishments. There is, however, a wide range of lodgings available: a couple of caravan parks offering camping and on-site vans, some pubs with cheap beds, and a fairly large number of motels, some of them, especially those on the way into town, quite reasonably priced.

Day 2   *Goulburn to Abercrombie River Camp*
(76 km/47 miles)

There is no fixed accommodation at Abercrombie River, making it suitable only for those of you carrying camping equipment. Accommodation is available at the pub in Taralga, leaving a tough 101 km ride to Jenolan Caves the following day.

Leaving Goulburn, you head toward the town of Taralga on the appropriately named Taralga Road. There are several ways of getting on to it, but the easiest is probably to head down Bourke St. (the road one back from the main street, Auburn St.), following it its full length. You pass by a church, several roundabouts, and the New South Wales Police Academy until eventually the road terminates. Here you turn right, bringing you out onto the Taralga road. If in doubt, ask a local.

Once on the Taralga road. the traffic is light and the surface is good, making for enjoyable cycling conditions as you pass through land that is reputedly one of the finest wool-growing areas in the world. The countryside rolls along, with a few minor hills to negotiate along the way.

After 45 km of cycling you arrive in Taralga, a small settlement that is the last town until Jenolan Caves. Bearing this is in mind, make sure you stock up at the general store and fill your water bags, as at the time of writing, despite the presence of a tap, there's no reliable drinking water at the Abercrombie River campsite.

Continue ahead out of town, signed for Wombeyan Caves. The terrain becomes a bit hillier than before, although there are no really significant climbs. The luxury of sealed road disappears at the 52 km mark, as you travel along a dirt road sandwiched between farmland. The surface is not too bad, but as always, take extra care to avoid straying into soft patches and potholes. The turnoff to the Wombeyan Caves is on the right at the 56 km point. It's about another 22 km down a dead-end road to the caves themselves, making this a detour for the dedicated cave enthusiast only. Still, if you're in the mood, there is some accommodation available there. On the left side of the road by the turnoff is a house with an eclectic assortment of weird items scattered around the front lawn.

After 65 km, the road thankfully becomes sealed again, making the going somewhat easier. Fine views out over a steep valley greet you 8 km later, the Abercrombie River lying somewhere far below. "Steep descent" signs by the roadside foreshadow some exhilarating riding ahead, and they're not wrong. The road plummets as it twists and turns down the valley wall. Unless you're the sort of person that prizes an adrenalin rush over personal well-being, you're likely to significantly shorten the life of your brake blocks here. After about 3 km you reach the valley floor and the Abercrombie River campsite.

To be honest, I was a little disappointed with the camping area when I first arrived. There's a dry toilet and some picnic tables, etc., but as far as I could tell, despite the presence of a tap, there is no drinking water, including the river, which in January was barely a trickle. Still, it's somewhere to pitch your tent, and the natural surroundings are pleasant enough.

Day 3. *Abercrombie River Camp to Jenolan Caves*
(70 km/43 miles)

It doesn't take long to realize that after the major descent down to the campsite, there's a pretty tough climb to negotiate in order to get out of the valley again. In fact, the climb out of Abercrombie River would have to rate as the steepest in this whole book, so steep at times that it in the absence of front panniers it becomes tough to keep the front wheel on the ground. Although the climb is extremely tough, fortunately it's not terribly long (although it feels it): 2.5 km from the campsite to the top of the rise. Once on top there's barely time to catch your breath before the sealed surface ends and you're back on the gravel.

You continue to gradually climb for some distance, eventually passing through an altitude of 1,000 m, a gain of some 300 m from the campsite. The road rises and falls as it passes through a pleasant mixture of native bushland and pine plantations, part of Gurnang State Forest. Although you're traveling on the Goulburn-Oberon road, you're unlikely to encounter more than a handful of cars all day, making the ride through the forest that much more enjoyable. The surface is generally pretty good (relatively speaking), especially if the weather has been dry. Along the way, various minor roads lead off from the main route you are following; ignore these and continue in the direction of Oberon until approximately 32 km from Abercrombie River you come to a fork in the road where there is a bridge over a stream known as Green Hill Creek.

Some maps indicate there is a campsite at this point, but after some scouting around under the bridge, I found only small traces of a site long since derelict. However, there are numerous places in the area where it would be possible to discretely pitch a tent. Take the unsealed road leading away to the right known as Shooters Hill Rd., the first 3 km of which are unsealed and, as I discovered, can become a bit messy when conditions are wet. Eventually you rejoin the sealed surface, and although it's a relief to be back on the bitumen, the sensation is short-lived, because approximately 10 km later at the 45 km mark, you turn right down an unsealed road signed to Ginkin. About 2 km down this road you join another forestry road, turning right then left, continuing to follow the Ginkin road., eventually coming out at a T-junction after 52 km. Turn left at the junction in the direction of Ginkin, which you reach 5 km or so down the road. The settlement is really just a couple of houses (no facilities), but serves as reassurance that you're on the right track. A little further down the road, there's a turnoff to the right signed to your final destination for the day, Jenolan Caves.

With energy levels replenished by the knowledge that you're in the home stretch, continue down the road, which at 63 km becomes sealed again, this time for the remainder of your journey. A short distance on, you come to an intersection where you turn left, signed to Jenolan Caves. This is where your descent and the fun begins. The road drops gradually at first, but before long you're at the edge of what seems like a massive hole in the ground, at the bottom of which lie the caves and the buildings of the resort. The whole area is lush and heavily wooded, adding to the spectacular beauty of the area. To get to the bottom you have to traverse a series of hair-raising hairpin bends that cling to the nearly vertical valley wall.

Eventually, at the bottom you're confronted with the splendid sight of the Jenolan Caves house complex, a grand example of a traditional Victorian lodge. If you can afford a bit of a splurge, I would strongly recommend that you treat yourself and get a room here. The rates aren't cheap, but the price does include a fine dinner and full breakfast, making this pretty good value overall. The only accommodation alternative near the caves is camping. Ask at the information center for details on where you're allowed to pitch your tent. There are also a couple of cabin-style establishments in the area, but you have to make the long climb up from the valley floor in order to reach them, making them impractical if you wish to check out the caves.

It's worth spending a day or two here to explore the caves themselves. There are several to have a look at, all part of a massive underground limestone cavern system that although open to the public since 1867, still contains sections that remain unexplored. The entrance to the caves lies under a massive natural limestone arch that spans the road, a spectacular sight in its own right. The whole area is magnificent, providing many possibilities for short walks and general exploring.

Day 4   *Jenolan Caves to Lithgow/Katoomba*
(Lithgow 55 km/34 miles; Katoomba 78 km/48 miles)

Today's ride offers alternative destinations in order to best cater for your own personal interests. Katoomba is the main base to exploring the Blue Mountains, being close to many of the area's more major attractions including the spectacular rock formation known as the Three Sisters. Katoomba also has a wide range of accommodation available. Unfortunately, the Great Western Highway on which Katoomba lies isn't really a suitable or safe road on which to cycle into Sydney, so I would suggest you throw your bike on a train into the city instead. Alternatively, you can backtrack to Mt. Victoria and link up with the old Bells Line of Road, a far more scenic and quieter route to Sydney's fringe. Cycling directly to Lithgow from Jenolan Caves instead of going to Katoomba puts you at the beginning of this road and provides a slightly shorter route overall.

Leaving the Natural Arch, it isn't long before you begin to climb. In contrast to the short, plunging descent of the road on the way in, the road out is more of a gradual incline. Rather than the painful ordeal you might expect it to be, I found the climb out to be surprisingly enjoyable and far easier than I anticipated. The narrow road clings to the valley wall, winding around as it rises, presenting you with changing and spectacular vistas that serve to distract your brain from the messages your hard-working legs are sending. After approximately 4 km of climbing, you arrive at the Mt. Inspiration lookout and the approximate halfway point of the ascent. At the lookout, take a breather, enjoy the natural beauty of the surroundings, and congratulate yourself on the significant altitude you have already gained.

The road continues to rise as before until it eventually levels out after 8.7 km. A place offering cabin accommodation is situated here on the left side of the road. Despite the road's leveling out somewhat, there's still another 8 km of slightly uphill travel before you reach a high spot of 1,250 m at the 17 km point. This is the highest you're going to be for the rest of the tour, meaning only one thing: it's downhill from here. And indeed it is—nothing hair raising, but a nice gentle descent allowing you to relax and enjoy some of the great scenery. Cycle past the turnoff to Oberon and continue ahead signed to Hampton (3 km), Lithgow (30 km), and Katoomba (52 km). All along this stretch there are some magnificent Blue Mountain views over on the right.

Hampton is a small place, mainly catering to motorists passing through on their way to Jenolan. There are a couple of establishments where you can sit, buy food and drink, and relax. After Hampton, despite the odd bump the road continues to be predominantly downward sloping as it follows a ridge line. Down below there are good views over fertile pastures, which even when I rode through in the middle of summer looked remarkably green and lush. As a native West Australian, this was a foreign sight to me, as back home nothing looks particularly lush in January.

Just after 40 km of cycling, you come to a fork in the road, and it's time to decide whether to head for Lithgow or Katoomba. The right fork is signed to Katoomba (36 km) and

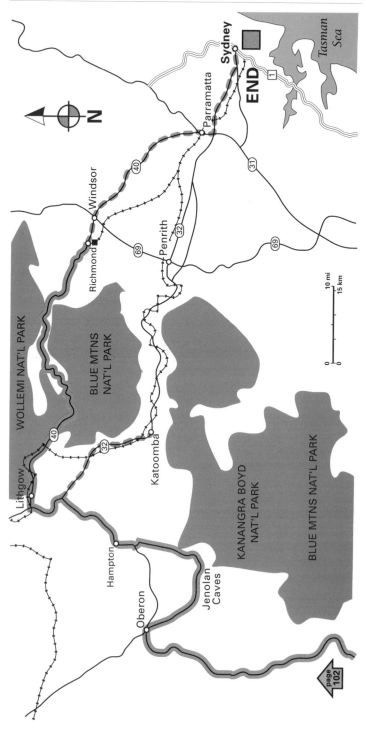

the left to Lithgow (14 km). This book describes the remainder of the route to Lithgow, but going to Katoomba is pretty straightforward anyway. It is briefly as follows. After about 7 km farther on Jenolan Caves Rd., you come out onto the rather busy Great Western Highway near Hartley. Here you turn right and follow the highway, passing through Blackheath and Medlow Bath before arriving in Katoomba after approximately 78 km of cycling for the day.

If heading for Lithgow, follow the left fork on what is predictably enough now called Lithgow Road. Before long you begin a fast and exhilarating 2 km descent down to the valley floor, where you cross a small bridge over Cox's River. As is most often the case, once you have descended into a valley you have to climb back out again, and this is no exception. At first the road winds as it climbs, but thankfully the gradient is not too severe, and all in all, the climb is not that tough. After a couple of km the road straightens as it continues to rise, eventually bringing you out onto the Great Western Highway at the 49 km mark. Turn left and cycle along the highway, which after a couple of days of nearly traffic-free cycling feels intimidatingly busy. Luckily, in almost no time at all you're in the outskirts of Lithgow, where a bicycle lane begins, making the remainder of your journey into the town far more relaxing. You turn right off the highway near a McDonalds, down a road that takes you into the center of town, passing the tourist information office on your way.

Lithgow, with a population of around 15,000, is a town with an interesting industrial past. Named in 1827, the town spawned a local coal mining industry, which supplied the needs of early railway construction. The arrival of the railway in 1869 sparked other ventures, including iron and steel industries (first steel produced in Australia), copper smelters, breweries, and brickworks. The Zig-Zag railway, consisting of a series of some 10 tunnels blasted out of the mountains, was hailed worldwide as an engineering marvel when completed in 1910. Unfortunately, various factors combined to erode Lithgow's early industrial promise, and now there are no working coal mines in the area, the last one closing in 1985. Still, several sites around town, including Blast Furnace Park, serve as reminders of the boom days and make for a worthwhile visit. Fortunately, the Zig-Zag railway is once again operational as a tourist railway and is one of the main attractions of the area.

There's quite a good choice of accommodation available in Lithgow, consisting of the usual mix of motels, well-priced pubs, and caravan parks. Fortunately, there is also a backpacker's hostel called Bent Backs at 45 Roy St., located quite close to the center of town. To get to it, turn left off Main St. onto Eskbank St., which becomes Roy St. The hostel is on the right-hand side just down the road from the post office. It's a small, quiet, family-run place located in what is essentially the proprietors' home, and perhaps while not the best hostel I've come across, it's friendly and undoubtedly offers the best budget alternative in town, especially if you're traveling alone.

Day 5   *Lithgow to Richmond* (Train to central Sydney) *(81 km/50 miles)*

This is the last leg of your Canberra to Sydney tour, a ride along the Old Bells Line of Road. through the magnificent Blue Mountains, finishing in Richmond, a settlement on the outer fringe of Sydney's suburban sprawl. As you would expect with mountain terrain, there are a few hills to negotiate along the route, but all your hard work is rewarded in the end by a magnificent descent from the mountains onto the coastal plain at the end of the ride.

Finding your way out of Lithgow is a fairly simple affair. Get onto Mort St., which runs parallel with Main St., and head east (most likely a left turn). Before long, Mort St. turns into the Old Bells Line of Road, the road you will be traveling on for the rest of the day. There isn't much time to shake off the morning cobwebs before you are confronted with a sizeable climb out of town up the promisingly named Scenic Hill. The gradient is fairly steep, but the worst of the climbing is over in approximately 2 km. Have a rest at the top and enjoy some good views of Lithgow below.

With the initial climb up Scenic Hill over, the bulk of the altitude for the day has been gained, and the road begins to roll along in a series of small climbs followed by small descents. Traffic along the road is moderately heavy and fast-moving, with a decent shoulder most of the time. Unfortunately, the shoulder periodically disappears as the road passes through rocky canyons where a path has been blasted through the mountains, so take care not to stray out too far onto the roadway. I rode this section on a Sunday when tourist traffic is probably at its worst, and it wasn't too bad, so you shouldn't really have any problems.

After about 10 km, you pass the railway siding of Clarence on the left side of the road. This is the departure point for the famous Zig-Zag railway, which makes its way down to Bottom Points, via an amazing zigzag track layout. Continuing on, there are some postcard Blue Mountain views over on the right as you cycle along. Valleys of dense bushland and craggy limestone outcrops make for numerous photo opportunities, although access to vantage points is often blocked by roadside crash barriers. At the 18 km mark you come to Bell, where the road from Mt. Victoria joins the Old Bells Line of Road. If you started the ride today from Katoomba instead of Lithgow, this is the point where you rejoin the tour. Apart from a roadhouse, there's nothing else at Bell to make you linger.

After about 35 km you begin your ascent of Mt. Tomah, which in terms of size and difficulty is probably comparable to the first climb of the day up Scenic Hill. You reach the top and an altitude of 1,000 m at the 38.5 km point, where a picnic spot with a couple of roadside shelters is a nice place to break for lunch and catch your breath. When I was at the top of Mt. Tomah, pockets of cloud were wafting across the road, and icy rain was falling. I would say that cycling along up there, I was the coldest I have ever been in Australia, and it was the middle of summer. If you've got the time, you can also check out the Mt. Tomah Botanic Gardens, which boast a fine collection of cool-climate plants, covering some 18 hectares.

With Mt. Tomah conquered, it's really pretty easy going for the rest of the day. There's also a noticeable change in the nature of your surroundings, with the rugged Blue Mountain scenery replaced by orchards. The road is pretty much a gradual downhill for the next 20 km or so, as you pass by numerous roadside stalls selling produce from the area's orchards. The fruit they offer, which in summer is mainly peaches and apples, is really a good value. Unfortunately, the fruit is often sold only in tray-size lots, making it difficult for a fully laden touring cyclist to carry. However, a couple of juicy peaches consumed by the roadside is heaven.

After passing through Bilpin, your downhill holiday is briefly interrupted at the 60 km point. Here you climb for a couple of km up to Kurrajong Heights and the top of Bellbird Hill, where your efforts are rewarded by some fine views out across the coastal plain. It is only here that you realize just how high you've been, and how far you have to descend.

Hard-won altitude is rapidly lost on the exhilarating descent down Bellbird Hill. A series of hairpin bends makes for some fantastic freewheeling fun, although you must exercise caution so as to not run too wide on the corners into the path of oncoming traffic. After one of the fastest 6 km you're likely to experience, the bulk of Bellbird is unfortunately over, and it's time once again to put some effort into pedaling. The remaining 10 km into Richmond is more or less flat, although traffic increases considerably as you approach the town, emphasizing why it's best to take a train for the trip into the city. The Richmond train station is easy to find, as it is located right next door to a McDonalds (always a useful landmark), on the left-hand side of the road just after a set of traffic lights.

Richmond lies at the end of the suburban rail network, with regular train services heading into the city. Traveling time varies depending on the train you catch, although it's likely to take about an hour to get to one of the city stations (Central, Town Hall, Circular Quay, and Wynyard). Remember when you buy your ticket that you also need one for your bike, which can be carried with you in any carriage.

Sydney

Almost 3.5 million people live in this beautiful, thriving, exciting, energetic world city. If you think this sounds a bit too enthusiastic to be true, just make your way down to Circular Quay on a bright sunny day and gaze at the Opera House and the bridge against the backdrop of the deep blue water of the harbor.

Sydney is Australia's oldest and largest city—the site of the first convict settlement in 1788. Throughout its roguish history, it grew up in a relatively unplanned fashion (in contrast to Canberra), which is probably one reason why it is so interesting. It has some great shops, restaurants, and beaches, and plenty of budget accommodation both in the central area and close to the beaches. Both of the official YHA hostels are located in Glebe, approximately 2.5 km from Central Station. Sydney also has a great climate and lots to see and do—no wonder it was chosen to host the Olympic Games in the year 2000.

To really get the feel of Sydney you should do a lot of walking and see some of the famous sights at the same time, places like Circular Quay and the Opera House, the Harbour Bridge and the Rocks—an historic area with some interesting specialty shops and restaurants—Hyde Park, the Botanic Gardens and the Domain, the Art Gallery, George St., and the Queen Victoria building. For a fantastic inexpensive trip on the water, take the regular ferry to Manly, an ocean suburb with nice beaches, coastal walks, and an old-fashioned seaside atmosphere. The trip takes about half an hour, and you'll see Sydney from some interesting angles and the Opera House at its best—it was designed to be seen from the water.

The futuristic monorail is worth a trip, and you might like to stop off at Darling Harbor, which was developed as a tourist area in the 1980s. Kings Cross is Sydney's famous/infamous nightlife and red-light area. There is undoubtedly a seamy side to the Cross, but it also has some good restaurants. Darlinghurst is a focal point for Sydney's gay population and has some fashionable restaurants, while trendy Paddington is a highly attractive area of old restored terraced houses, galleries, pubs, restaurants, and bookshops.

Getting around Sydney is pretty easy. There is a good suburban train system with a central city circle, which has

What's a book about Australia without a photo of Sydney's famous modern Opera House, on the shores of the harbor?

trains running every couple of minutes. There are also ferries, the monorail, and buses to various points.

A brief sketch like this can't possibly do justice to fabulous Sydney, but I hope it will encourage you to explore the city's many interesting possibilities.

Chapter 10.
Sydney to Brisbane

This pedal-powered exploration of Australia's east coast between Sydney and Brisbane has something for everyone. Magnificent beaches and coastal scenery, picturesque towns, lush pastures, timbered hills, national parks, and World Heritage–listed rain forests are just a few of the attractions you'll encounter  along the way. Although a fairly lengthy tour, the terrain is largely cycle-friendly, and the ever-changing mix of coastal and inland scenery, becoming increasingly lush and tropical as you head north, ensures enjoyable touring. Highlights include Newcastle, Port Stephens, the bats of Wingham and Bellingen, Dorrigo National Park, Coffs Harbour, weirdly wonderful Nimbin, the Gold Coast, and Tamborine Mountain, just to mention a few.

If you're short of time, many of the towns on the route are situated on the main Sydney-Brisbane rail line, allowing you to customize the tour to suit your needs. Coffs Harbour, situated almost at the halfway point of the tour, would make a good alternative start/finish destination.

Start	Gosford or Newcastle
Finish	Beenleigh (Brisbane) or Gold Coast
Distance	1,039 km/644 miles (Gosford to Beenleigh)
Duration	3 weeks (15 cycling days, including 6 half-days).
Terrain	This route is predominantly flat in coastal regions, with hillier sections inland. There are notable climbs near Comboyne, Bowraville, and Tamborine Mountain.
Road Conditions	The majority of cycling is on quiet country roads with occasional stints on the busier Pacific Highway. The route also contains several

sections of unsealed road, generally in good
condition apart from the stretch between
Bombah Point and the Seal Rocks road, where
an alternative route is given.

Accomm.   A good variety of accommodation is available
along the route, including motels, pubs, and
caravan parks. There are also youth hostels in
many of the towns visited.

Route Description

In order to escape the heavy traffic and unfriendly cycle-
touring conditions of Sydney's suburbs, I suggest that you
jump on one of the regular trains from Central station and
head north to either Gosford or Newcastle to begin this tour.
Gosford is the closer of the two towns to Sydney, lying less
than 100 km to the north. However, a large part of the ride
from Gosford to Newcastle is along the Pacific Highway, and
although it's not a bad road to cycle on (the bulk of the traffic
travels on the Newcastle Freeway), it isn't particularly exciting
either. But if you want to start from as close to Sydney as is
safe, Gosford is a good choice. Alternatively, you can skip the
first part of this tour by catching the train directly to
Newcastle, New South Wales's second-biggest city, located
167 km north of Sydney and a destination worth exploring in
its own right.

Day 1   Sydney (train to Gosford) to Budgewoi
half day (38 km/22 miles cycling)

The train to Gosford takes just over an hour, but the time
passes quickly as you travel through some terrific scenery
along the way. Beyond Sydney's suburbs, the train rattles
through Ku Ring Gai Chase National Park, over the beautiful
Hawkesbury Inlet, and through Brisbane Water National Park
before finally pulling into Gosford station.

Once out of the station, you may want to pay a visit to the
tourist information office, which is located directly outside at
the edge of a shady little park. After you've explored all that
Gosford has to offer, leave town by cycling south (turn right)
along the road adjacent to the station. Before long, turn left
on a road signed to Terrigal and the Entrance. I was expecting
this coastal stretch of road around Lake Tuggerah to be fairly

quiet when I first rode it, but unfortunately the traffic was nonstop all the way. This was undoubtedly due in part to the school holidays and the late afternoon hour, but I should think that even at the best of times you could expect a lot of vehicles. The first few km out of Gosford are fairly hilly, but before too long, things begin to flatten out. Ignore a road leading off to the right signed to Terrigal and continue ahead toward the Entrance.

Despite pockets of bushland, much of the scenery consists of housing estates and other coastal developments. After just over 18 km, you reach the place with the intriguing name of the Entrance, where a major road leads off to the left. Continue ahead, however, toward Toukley. Once at Toukley, turn right off the main road and head over a bridge in the direction of Budgewoi, which is reached a short distance later after approximately 38 km of cycling for the day. Although only a small center, Budgewoi has a motel and a caravan park. For something a little different you can camp in the Munmorah State Recreation Area about 5 km out of town, although it's not really any cheaper than the caravan park. Take the turnoff to the right signed to the State Recreation Area as you come into Budgewoi. After a couple of km you pass the national park office, which if open may decide to charge you a park usage fee. With a little bit of arguing, however, I've found that the majority of the time when you're cycling you can get the ranger to overlook this fee, and rightly so. Continue on past the office for about a km, then look for a small road leading off to the right. Take this road, which eventually brings you to Freemans camping area, located in a pretty, secluded location by the ocean. There's a toilet block and cold-water showers as well as some fire grates and ready-chopped fire wood. Camping here is not free, and you should expect a visit from a park official, who will charge you around $10 per site.

Day 2   *Budgewoi/Newcastle to Nelson Bay*
(95 km/52 km from Budgewoi;
59 miles/32 miles from Newcastle)

From Budgewoi, make your way to the Pacific Highway. If you stayed at Freemans camping area, you can save yourself some backtracking by turning right instead of left, back the way you came, about a km from the campsite. After about 3 km pleasant riding through bushland, you come out on the

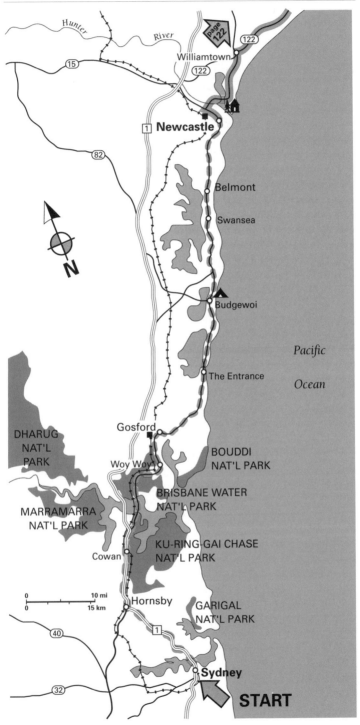

considerably busier Pacific Highway, where you turn right in the direction of Newcastle. As previously mentioned, much of the Sydney-Newcastle traffic now travels on the faster Newcastle Freeway, with the result that although busy, traffic on the Pacific Highway is definitely bearable. The Pacific Highway runs all the way up to Brisbane, and although avoided where possible, you will travel on it again a couple of times during the remainder of this tour. Fortunately, the highway has a very wide, lane-width shoulder, making cycling on it fast and fairly enjoyable.

After 17 km you come to the town of Swansea with quite a good selection of shops, which makes it a good place to stop for breakfast. The highway rolls along, and there are a number of climbs to negotiate and downhills to enjoy, although nothing too major. As you approach the outskirts of Newcastle, the wide shoulder erodes to nothing, making cycling a little hair raising at times, but before long, after a nice descent and approximately 43 km, you find yourself in the heart of the city. Newcastle is a center well worth exploring, and if you are not in a hurry you may want to call it a day and have a look around.

Newcastle is New South Wales's second-biggest city, with a population of around 260,000, and is a major industrial and commercial center. Located at the mouth of the Hunter River, Newcastle is a revitalized city with many magnificent old buildings restored to original condition. Tragically, in 1989 Newcastle was the site of Australia's most damaging earthquake, resulting in 12 deaths and extensive property damage. The city has recovered well, although some buildings around town still bear the scars. The city also has some fantastic surfing beaches close to the center of town.

There are numerous accommodation options, as you would expect in a city of this size, with a good selection of hotels, motels, pubs, caravan parks (at Stockton), and a couple of backpacker places, including a YHA hostel. To get to it, turn left out of the train station on Scott St., and take the second right down Pacific St. The YHA (Irene Hall) is on Pacific St. just over Hunter St. on the right-hand side.

To leave Newcastle, jump aboard a passenger ferry over to Stockton, a 5-minute trip over the Hunter River. The ferry departs from Queens Wharf, which is located near the train station, its modern design and tower making it easy to find. The charge for the ferry is minimal, and bikes travel for free. Once in Stockton, cycle straight ahead and down the main street. Before long the road runs parallel with the beach, with some good views over the ocean to your right. A short distance on, the road curves around to the left, and you turn left down Stone St. in order to join the main road to Williamstown. From here the massive BHP Steelworks and traffic bridge over the Hunter River are clearly visible.

The Williamstown road is pretty much flat and straight, with a moderate amount of traffic, increasing late in the afternoon as people make their way home from work. There isn't terribly much to see, although the thunderous roar of F-18 fighter jets taking off from the RAAF base near Williamstown is sure to interrupt your daydreaming. If you are into aircraft, there's a museum called Fighter World located on the base, which is probably worth a look. For a break from the traffic, turn left at the 68 km point (25 km from Newcastle), down Marsh Rd. It's the next road after the one signed to Lemon Tree Passage, with the turnoff situated just past a gas station. The road is a hodgepodge of repairs, with the surface resembling a patchwork quilt of filled-in potholes, and although a little rough at times, it is generally good to cycle on, being practically devoid of traffic. As the name suggests, the road runs through soggy-looking marshland for much of its 8 km, rejoining the main road at the 76 km point, where you turn left, signed to Nelson Bay (15 km).

Numerous times during the final km into Nelson Bay, I expected to see the town around the next corner, only to be confronted with more open road. Eventually, after a small climb and 92 km of cycling for the day, you descend past luxury holiday homes and into town, catching sight of the magnificent sapphire-blue waters of Port Stephens in the process. Make your way down to the waterfront where the tourist information office is located, for detailed information on accommodation and activities. The YHA hostel is located in the Shoal Bay motel, about 2 km from the center of town. To get there, just follow Shoal Bay Rd., which runs in front of the tourist information office, for a couple of km. The motel that houses the hostel is located on the waterfront, just up from a caravan park, with a beautiful swimming beach across the road. The hostel itself, although a little makeshift, is small and comfortable, its greatest asset being its proximity to a fantastic beach.

Day 3   **Nelson Bay to Forster**
             (85 km/105 km or 53 miles/65 miles, alternate routes)

Leaving Nelson Bay involves no cycling, but rather an enjoyable 1-hour trip across beautiful Port Stephens by passenger ferry to the small settlement of Tea Gardens. Cycling out of Nelson Bay would involve an enormous back-track, back almost as far as Williamstown, making the ferry the only sensible method of departure. The ferry makes a crossing three times a day, the earliest departure time of 9:00 A.M. providing sufficient time to comfortably cover the distance to Forster. If you miss the ferry or for some reason it isn't operating, as was the case when I needed it (mechanical problems), you can catch a ride with one of the tourist boats that also operate out of the marina, although this is likely to prove a more costly alternative. The ferry departs from the jetty located in front of the tourist information center.

Once in Tea Gardens, cycle over the bridge joining the town to Hawks Nest. This structure, known as the singing bridge because of the noise it makes when the wind whistles through the railings, was built in 1974 for the considerable sum then of $3.5 million, as part of a project to build another major coastal road in order to alleviate some of the pressure on the busy Pacific Highway. After some lobbying by environmental groups, however, the project was scrapped, leaving behind a very expensive bridge that today literally links nowhere to nowhere. Once over the bridge, continue ahead for a short distance before turning left at a T-junction near a golf course, signed to Myall Lakes National Park. For those of you who have been studying your maps, a pleasant surprise awaits as you enter the park: the road is smooth and sealed. As this has only been done fairly recently, most maps still show one of those broken lines that most cyclists dread.

Myall Lakes National Park is home to one of the few remaining coastal lake systems in NSW, and is home to an interesting combination of pristine lakes and coastal beaches, the road for much of the way sandwiched between the two. The park also surprisingly contains small patches of litoral rain forest, adapted to survive in the harsh coastal environment. Once inside the borders of the national park, the road is smooth and flat and practically devoid of traffic, making for some wonderful cycling. The scenery is a mixture

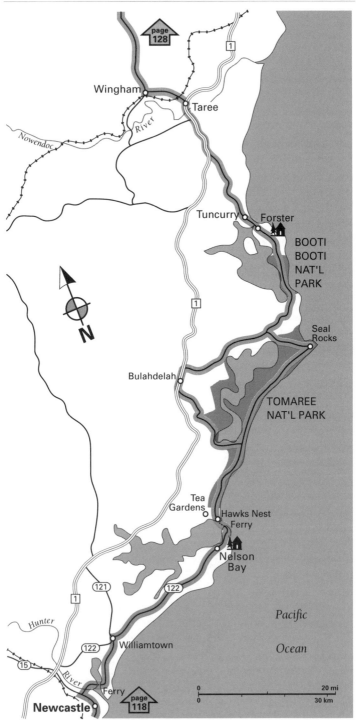

of coastal vegetation and ferns, with glimpses of tall dunes away to your right, a reminder of your proximity to the ocean.

Twenty-two km from Tea Gardens, a small road on the left leads down to Mungo Brush, a camping area operated by the National Parks and Wildlife Service. It's only about a 100 m off the road and is situated on the edge of the lake known as Bombah Broadwater. Even if you don't intend to stay here, it's probably a good idea to fill your water bottles, especially if the weather is warm. Just up from Mungo Brush, you come across the first pockets of rain forest, an intriguing sight considering the apparent dryness of the surrounding vegetation. Trees such as native olive, brush bloodwood, and cabbage-leaf palms are just a few of the species to be found. Several more camping areas are strung out over several km from Mungo Brush, providing an accommodation option if time is getting on or you just want to take it easy.

At the 26.5 km point, you come to a junction where you have the option to either turn left or continue ahead, depending on your liking for rugged terrain. Turning left provides a smoother but longer route to Forster via Bulahdelah, whereas continuing straight ahead takes you along a very rough and rocky track toward Seal Rocks, but shortens your journey by more than 20 km. The Seal Rocks route is very rough and is probably only suitable for people on mountain bikes.

If you decide to turn left, it's not long before you have to hop on one of the few remaining cable ferries in NSW, which takes you over to Bombah Point (operates between 8:00 A.M.–6:00 P.M.) where there's a restaurant and a shop. From Bombah Point, it's about another 16 km to the Pacific Highway and the town of Bulahdelah. You leave the highway after only a short while (after approximately 44 km), turning right onto the road known as the Lakes Way, which takes you the rest of the way to Forster.

If you continue ahead up the track to Seal Rocks, be prepared for some tough going. Although the route is pretty much flat, it's strewn with rocks the size of soccer balls, making for slow going and some bone-jarring jolts, making you wish you were on a fully suspended mountain bike. This obstacle course of a track stretches for almost exactly 20 km, finally bringing you out onto a sealed road that feels like heaven. Away to the right is the small coastal community of Seal Rocks, where it is possible to camp. To get to Forster, turn left, joining the Lakes Way after 5 km at Bungwahl.

Once on the Lakes Way, although there are some hills around, conditions are generally conducive to some fairly fast cycling, with some nice views over Smiths and Wallis Lakes enhancing the experience. After passing through Pacific Palms, you cycle by a couple of caravan parks before eventually reaching the outskirts of Forster after about 85 km or 105 km, depending on your choice of route.

The twin towns of Forster and Tuncurry (pop. 16,000) lie at the entrance to Wallis Lake, boasting some fine beaches and offering access to various water sports. The town is probably most well known for the ironman distance triathlon it hosts every year. The race attracts many of the world's premier triathletes, some of whom may greet you as they zip past on their space-age super bikes. There's a good variety of accommodation available in town including a very nice YHA hostel called Forster Dolphin lodge, which is located in a converted motel complex. To get to it, just continue along the road that brought you into town for as far as you can go. Eventually it terminates at a T-junction by the coast, where you turn left. The hostel is on the right-hand side of the road about 100 m or so up from the turnoff, next to a modern-looking block of apartments.

Day 4   Forster to Wingham
half-day (48 km/30 miles)

Today's ride is relatively short, giving you a chance to recover from the fairly long leg into Forster. It takes you away from the coast and the busy Pacific Highway, inland to Wingham, a nice little place with a fantastic flying fox colony worthy of exploration.

Leave Forster by crossing over the bridge to Tuncurry, continuing ahead on the road signed to Taree. I was a little surprised by the volume of traffic traveling along this stretch of road, but it was the middle of summer and is probably subject to fairly large seasonal variation. There's a decent shoulder for the first few km, but it soon disappears, replaced instead by a crumbling edge. The terrain gets progressively hillier the closer you get to the Pacific Highway, although there are no climbs of any real significance. I generally find it quite nice to get back into a few hills after days of flat coastal cycling. Most people, noncyclists especially, imagine cycling heaven to be perfectly flat, but for me a few good climbs and especially descents serve to break up and enhance the journey. The anticipation of the view from the top of a hill, or a vista waiting beyond the next corner, spurs me on. Cycling hell, in my opinion, would have to be a perfectly flat, perfectly straight road with tons of traffic, 40°C heat, no views and a 30-knot headwind.

The Forster road meets the Pacific Highway after about 23 km, where you turn right to join it for a short stint into Taree. The highway is generally fairly good to cycle on, with a wide shoulder the bulk of the way. Several roadside rest areas designed to revive fatigued motorists also provide good stopping points for fatigued cyclists. At one such area at about the 28 km point, I remember pulling over for a snack and a nice lie-down in the sun, only to be awakened by the presence of an enormous monitor lizard strolling by. It was the biggest lizard I've ever seen and must have been well over a meter in length. I nearly jumped 10 feet in the air when I first saw it, but it seemed disinterested. It disappeared into the bush, leaving me fumbling with my camera.

After approximately 35 km, you cross a bridge over the Manning River and arrive in the town of Taree, a decent-size place with a good selection of shops and accommodation. Stop for lunch or even stay overnight; either way, Wingham is not very far away. To get there, continue ahead after crossing the bridge that brings you into Taree, down Commerce St., which after passing through a couple of suburbs turns into the Wingham road. I was surprised when cycling down this road by just how tropical and lush everything seemed to be. Looking out over bright green fields and the occasional palm tree to distant hills, the air thick with humidity, you could be forgiven for thinking you were in far north Queensland, when in fact you're still closer to Sydney than to Brisbane. The 13 km or so to Wingham is soon covered, leaving you with a good amount of time to relax off the bike and give the legs a chance to recover from the exertions of the tour so far.

Wingham is an attractive little town with several fine old buildings gathered around a central reserve. The real attraction of the place, however, would have to be the small pocket of rain forest at the bottom end of town known as Wingham Brush. Over the summer months, this lush outcrop of vegetation is home to tens of thousands of flying foxes, often known as fruit bats. As you walk along a series of pathways constructed to allow you to explore the forest without damaging it, a number of plaques provide interesting information about the bats and some of the numerous other inhabitants of Wingham Brush, and about the forest itself, which was restored from a state of decay to the fine shape it's in today. Although the bats are harmless, it's still quite an eerie sensation to walk alone through the dense vegetation, as thousands of bats hang in the branches and flap through the air above.

Accommodation can be found in Wingham in the motel or in either of the local pubs. I stayed in the Australian hotel on Bent St., and found it to be a good value (breakfast included), providing the sort of basic but comfortable room typical of most country pubs.

Day 5   Wingham to Wauchope
(80 km/50 miles)

Today's ride travels predominantly on quiet back roads that take you into the lush hills around Comboyne, before a substantial descent back down to Wauchope. Much of the day's climbing is done on unsealed roads, making this one of the toughest but best days of the tour.

Leave Wingham by crossing over the railway lines and turning right, signed to Comboyne. Before long you're back out in the lush countryside on a nice quiet, sealed road, getting ever closer to the looming hills that you must tackle before the day is done. The road rolls along with a few small climbs to negotiate, but nothing serious. After about 12 km it's time to say goodbye to the sealed surface as it gives way to gravel, not returning until almost in Comboyne. The gravel surface, though rough in comparison to bitumen, is generally fairly good, although intermittent deep pockets of gravel that are difficult to spot until you are almost in them make cycling hazardous at times. I found this out the hard way, crashing heavily after hitting a gravel patch while going downhill. Out of all the thousands of km I cycled while researching this book, this was my only real fall. I managed to put my hands out, but my head still struck the ground and a rock heavily, leaving a large dent in my helmet. Had I not been wearing gloves and a helmet, things could have been messy, but luckily, although badly shaken I emerged relatively unscathed. The moral is: be careful.

At the 20 km mark, a sign by the side of the road signaling a narrow, winding road ahead gives some indication of the climb to come. From this point it's pretty much uphill for the next 12 km. The going is fairly tough, with the steep gradient and unsealed surface combining to make life difficult. As you get higher and higher, the view over the lush valley below gets better and better, providing a well-deserved reward for your efforts. The scenery along the road itself is also fantastic, with native forest and ferns providing welcome shade from the summer sun. After 28 km you come across a roadside picnic area, and then a km or so later, both providing good spots to break and have lunch. From the second picnic spot, there's a brief downhill before you resume climbing, reaching the real summit after 32.5 km at the turnoff to the Mt. Gibraltar lookout.

Continuing on, the road begins to descend, leveling out a short distance after the turnoff to Ellenborough Falls at the 34 km mark. The bulk of downhill fun is to be had later when descending from the Comboyne plateau, beyond the town itself. After rejoining the sealed surface at the 36.5 km point, the remaining 5 km into the small settlement of Comboyne is relatively easy going. Once in town you'll find a couple of small stores where you can buy lunch. Also, if you intend to stay at the Rainbow Ridge hostel, it's probably a good idea to purchase a few supplies here as well because the hostel is actually situated quite a distance from the town of Wauchope.

Once out of town, there are a couple of km of rolling road through pleasant farmland to negotiate before the real descent down from the plateau begins at the 47 km point, marked by a sign warning of the winding road ahead. Hard-won altitude is quickly lost as you gain momentum down the considerable slope. There are some fine views off to the left down into the valley below, but don't become too distracted, as there are several high-speed bends to negotiate along the way. After an exhilarating 6 km, the terrain levels out again as you cross over the Hardy's Creek bridge, and it's not long before you encounter a few small climbs. After 57 km you pass through the small outpost of Byabarra, where a roadside stall provides you with the opportunity to purchase a drink.

The road continues to roll along, eventually joining the Oxley Highway at the 68 km mark, where you turn right in the direction of Wauchope. From this point, away to the right, you can see a large rocky outcrop known as Rainbow Ridge, reminiscent of some of the formations in the magnificent Blue Mountains. The Rainbow Ridge hostel is located about 100 m up from the turnoff on the left side of the road. It's reasonably priced, but I'm not sure how much longer it will be open. When I stayed there I was the only guest, and by the look of

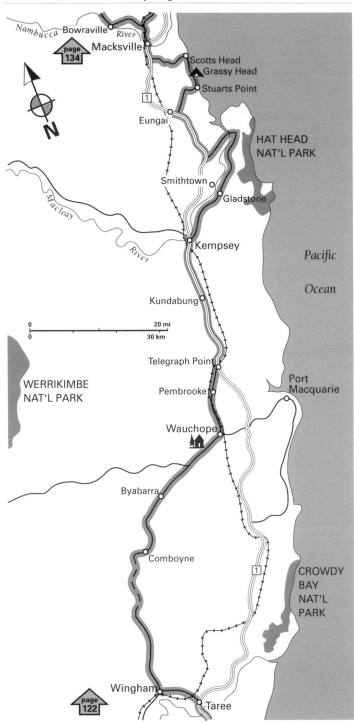

the visitors' book, the only one for quite a while. Anyway, if you want some peace and quiet, it's ideal.

From the hostel it's another 11 km along the Oxley Highway into the town of Wauchope itself. You pass Timbertown, an historical theme park, on the right-hand side of the road as you come into town. Also while in Wauchope, keep your eyes open for the "Big Bull," another grotesque but fun example of the passion of Australian country towns for erecting gigantic replicas of local livestock, flora, and fauna. Accommodation in Wauchope is available either in the motel or at the campground.

Day 6   Wauchope to Kempsey
half-day (54 km/33.5 miles)

Today's ride is another relatively short one, the first half along a quiet back road and the second along the Pacific Highway to the reasonably large town of Kempsey. There is also the option of staying overnight at South West Rocks or Trial Bay Gaol, an alternative that will add about 36 km to your journey.

Leave Wauchope by getting on the road to Telegraph Point, via Pembroke. This can be done by turning left near an auto parts shop onto Beechwood Rd. After almost 5 km of cycling, you cross over a bridge and come to a T-junction where you turn right, signed to Telegraph Point. The road is predominantly flat and quiet, flanked by state forest on the right and the main Sydney-Brisbane rail line on the left. At the 12 km mark, you cross under the railway lines and a short distance later come to a park in Pembroke where there is a nice picnic area with drinking water available. Finally, after 21 km of pleasant cycling on quiet roads, you reach the Pacific Highway once more, where you turn left in the direction of Kempsey.

The shoulder on this stretch of the highway is generally quite good, but as always, it varies considerably in terms of both width and surface quality, often disappearing on bridges all together. There's quite a long climb after 29 km over the Cooperabung range. Typical of highway climbs it's gradual, long, and straight, making it seem as if the top is never getting any closer. In comparison to many of the climbs of the tour so far, however, it's really only a fairly minor hill that shouldn't cause any problems.

As you approach the outskirts of Kempsey there's a nice picnic area off to the right, and not long after at the 49 km point, you pass the turnoff to Crescent Head, where a road sign reads "Crescent Head 19 km, Rio di Janeiro 12,000 km," something for all you world tourers to contemplate. You pass quite a few motels on the outskirts of town (apparently the cheapest), before crossing a bridge over the Macleay River and into Kempsey. It's quite a large town and these days is probably most famous as the home of the Akubra hat factory, making the hats that are synonymous with the Australian bush. Accommodation-wise there are numerous motels, caravan parks, and even pubs advertising backpacker-style accommodation in town. For a meal, try the RSL (Returned Services League) club down on the riverfront near the bridge. As a rule, RSL clubs offer attractively priced meals and drinks, although you will generally have to sign in as a guest before entering the premises.

If you'd prefer to stay out of town and are feeling energetic, you might want to camp out at Trial Bay Gaol, a 36 km ride north of Kempsey. Built on a headland, the gaol served as a civil prison in the 19th century and housed German prisoners of war during World War I. Nowadays it's open to the public and is surrounded by a nice camping area. You can also stay at nearby South West Rocks. If you decide to do this, you can rejoin the main tour the next day at Clybucca.

Day 7   *Kempsey to Macksville /Nambucca Heads (79 km/49 miles to Macksville; 91 km/59 miles to Nambucca Heads/)*

Leave Kempsey by retracing your steps over the bridge into town, and turn left off the Pacific Highway down the road signed to Gladstone, Hat Head, and South West Rocks. After a small initial climb, the countryside soon flattens out and the cycling is easy along a quiet road flanked by open grazing land.

After about 13 km, you cross a bridge over the Belmore River into the small settlement of Gladstone. A couple of km up the road, you take a left over another bridge, this time spanning the Macleay River, crossing over into Smithtown on the opposite bank. Find your way down to the road that runs along the riverfront, and cycle along it heading away from town (north). If only all roads were like this one. Cycling along the Summer Island road is pure joy. It's flat and without traffic, hugging the banks of the broad, blue Macleay River, farmland off to the left and looming fat hills in the distance. The only other people you're likely to encounter are those lucky souls whiling away the hours on the grassy riverbank, fishing rod in hand. After an all too short 10 km you come to a T-junction and join a busier road, turning left in the direction of Clybucca and the Pacific Highway. If you want to go to Southwest Rocks or Trial Bay Gaol, turn right here instead.

You rejoin the familiar Pacific Highway after 30 km of cycling, where you turn right. A short distance up the road you come to the Clybucca roadhouse. It's one of the more impressive roadhouses I've encountered, having a large dining area and shop, but its best features are around the back. In addition to having some nice showers, it has a swimming pool (free), and a nice one at that. They mainly cater to the scores of truck drivers that ply the route, but cycle tourers are also welcome. On the particular day I arrived it was oppressively hot, so it didn't take too much prompting to get me in. The cooling effect of the breeze on my skin as I cycled away felt fantastic. I wholeheartedly recommend the experience.

There's about 11 km of highway cycling to endure before you reach the turnoff to Stuarts Point on your right-hand side at the 44 km mark. You can continue along the highway if you want to shorten your journey, but in my opinion taking the back roads is worthwhile. The terrain becomes slightly hillier as you head toward the coast and Stuarts Point, where you turn left in the direction of Grassy Head at the 53.5 km point, just before you reach a group of shops (including a tavern). The road is quiet, passing through what is probably best described as coastal scrub. A few km down the road, you come to the turnoff to the Grassy Head Reserve, where there is a caravan and camping area, and a track leading down to the beach. It's only a few hundred meters off the road and is a good place to replenish your water bottles and take a break on the beach.

From Grassy Head, the road twists and turns, and there are several short but steep climbs to endure. Along this stretch of road you encounter a banana plantation, the first of many you'll see during the remainder of the tour. Bananas, mangoes, and avocadoes are all grown commercially in northern NSW, so you'll often come across roadside stalls where you can buy them plantation-fresh at very good prices. The road comes out at a T-junction at the 62.5 km point, where you turn left back toward the highway. The traffic increases slightly but is still fairly light as you cycle through rolling countryside, eventually passing under the highway before doubling back to rejoin it after 72 km.

After turning left onto the highway, it's not long before you reach the outskirts of Macksville (pop. 2,400), a sizeable town with a good selection of accommodation. It is possible to stay here instead of Nambucca Heads and may even be preferable if you're just spending the one night, because although Macksville is the less appealing of the two towns generally, in terms of distance it is closer to Bellingen, and lets you avoid the final stretch of highway to Nambucca Heads, which is particularly unpleasant. It's a tough decision; the main factor influencing my decision to press on to Nambucca Heads was the presence of a youth hostel. If you decide to stay, the next day, turn left once over the bridge spanning the Nambucca River in the direction of Bowraville. To get to Nambucca Heads, continue straight on along the highway.

The final 12 km stretch along the highway would have to rate as one of the least enjoyable sections in this book, as the road is both narrow and busy. The route is quite flat, however, and fortunately the km pass by quickly, the turnoff to Nambucca Heads coming at the 88 km point. The road winds around the coast and passes by the local RSL club (check it out for a cheap meal), before one last climb brings you into the center of town.

Nambucca Heads is a small resort town offering a range of activities, including fishing, windsurfing, or just lazing on the beach. There are also some great coastal views from the headland above the river mouth. There's a range of accommodation available, including a couple of reasonably priced motels and a good backpackers predictably called Nambucca backpackers, located at 3 Newman St., not far from the center of town. If you have difficulty finding it, just look for the markers on the street signs. It's probably a good idea to call ahead, as the hostel can get quite busy, Nambucca Heads being one of the more popular stopping-off points for travelers on the Sydney-Brisbane bus route.

Day 8   *Nambucca Heads to Bellingen*
half-day (50 km/31 miles)

This is a short but hilly ride inland on quiet back roads through some great countryside, ending in a town that in my opinion has to be one of the nicest I've come across.

Leave Nambucca Heads by taking the road that runs past the train station, back toward the highway, continuing straight ahead in the direction of Bowraville. After almost 5 km, as you cycle through Nambucca State Forest, you come to an intersection where you turn right signed to Bowraville. Continuing on, you come to yet another intersection after about 10 km, where you again turn right in the direction of Bowraville, joining a rolling road passing through pleasant green pastoral land.

You reach the final turnoff to Bowraville after 19 km when you arrive at a fork in the road, the town lying about a km away to the left. Unless you wish to go into town to have a look around or buy a drink, turn right at the fork in the direction of Bellingen. There are some nice views across to the Dorrigo Plateau at this point. After the fork in the road, there are a couple of longish gradual climbs to negotiate, before you again bear right at another fork, right to Bellingen, left to Missabotti at the 25 km point. A sign warning that the road is unsuitable for articulated vehicles gives some indication that there are a couple of hills still to be tackled. Not far from the turnoff, just after crossing a creek, the road becomes unsealed and you start to climb up what is known locally as Big Bowraville. The quiet little winding road passes through some magnificent stands of timber interspersed with clumps of lush tree ferns, providing plenty of great places to stop and catch your breath if the rather lengthy climb becomes too hard. After conquering the initial climb, you drop down into a gully before ascending yet again, although this climb is not quite as big as the first.

After about 36 km the road surface changes to loose gravel, which can be a little slippery in places, so it is good to join the sealed road once again a couple of km later. Once back on the sealed road, the remaining 14 km into Bellingen are fairly easy going. You make a right turn at a roundabout after 48 km and finish the ride with a nice descent into town.

Located alongside the Bellinger River, Bellingen is a fantastic mix of the old and the new. Traditional country surroundings and heritage buildings, combined with the artistic, hippy influence of those who come to the north coast seeking an alternative lifestyle, make for an appealing combination. In addition to the usual array of shops, the main street boasts art galleries, cafes, and other specialty stores, housed within handsome old premises. To top it all off, Bellingen has one of the finest backpacker establishments I

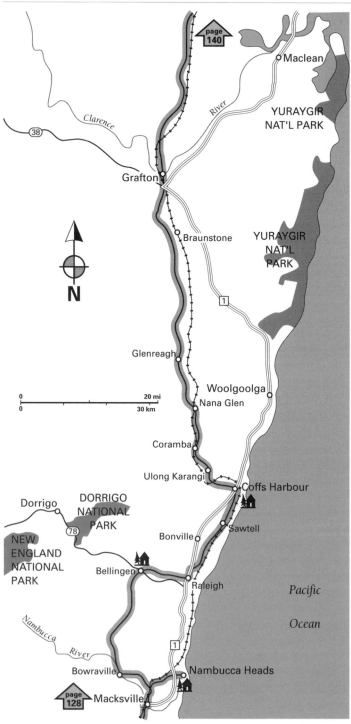

have ever stayed in. It's called Belfry lodge or Bellingen backpackers and is located just back from the main street on Short St. It's run by a friendly young couple who did a magnificent job of restoring the old timber building that houses the hostel. I liked it so much that, although I was on a tight schedule, my intended overnight stay somehow ended up lasting three days.

There are also some wonderful natural attractions in the surrounding area, including a flying fox colony and the beautiful, World Heritage–listed Dorrigo National Park. If you stay at the hostel, you can arrange to get a lift up to the national park, where the rain forest walks and visitors' center are worthy of the best part of a day's exploration. You could cycle there, but it's a tough 25 km slog uphill practically all the way.

Day 9   Bellingen to Coffs Harbor
half-day (39 km/24 miles)

Cycle out of Bellingen by taking the road next to the post office and crossing a bridge over the Bellinger River. Once over the bridge, continue ahead to a roundabout where you turn right, back toward the coast and the Pacific Highway. The road is best described as a country lane, narrow and twisting, but practically devoid of traffic. It's a delight to cycle on, running parallel to the Bellinger River, with some pleasant views across the green Bellinger Valley. There are a few small hills to tackle along the way, but nothing significant. Unfortunately, the tranquillity of your surroundings is shattered as you once again join the Pacific Highway at the 14 km point, turning left in the direction of Coffs Harbour.

This section of the highway is not particularly bike-friendly, generally being very busy and fairly narrow, which is a shame, as it passes through some nice countryside including patches of state forest. The first opportunity to get off the highway arrives at the 27 km mark, where you turn right down Lyons Rd. in the direction of Sawtell. The turnoff is at the crest of a hill. Continue down this road for a couple of km before taking a left, signed to Coffs Harbour. By now you are more or less cycling through suburbs and fairly heavy traffic, but luckily you can take advantage of a good- quality cycle path running most of the length of the road. After passing the airport on your right-hand side, you eventually come to a roundabout, where a left turn brings you to the center of town.

Coffs Harbour, with a population of around 45,000, is the biggest town on the central north coast. It has quite a large commercial center, as well as a number of good beaches. It's also on the main Sydney-Brisbane rail route, so it makes a good start/finish point if you don't have time to do the whole tour. One of the more famous attractions in town is the "Big Banana," a giant yellow tribute to the fruit grown commercially in the area. It's housed within a plantation where all your questions about the banana business can be answered. To get there, just cycle north up the highway for a couple of km.

There's a wide range of accommodation in town, including two hostels: Aussitel Backpackers Hostel at 312 High St., which is down toward the harbor, and the YHA hostel, Albany Lodge at 110 Albany St., which is pretty close to the center of town.

Day 10   Coffs Harbour to Grafton
(85 km/53 miles)

Today's ride sees you heading inland to Glenreagh and on to Grafton, a picturesque town located on the Clarence River. The route is quite hilly at times, especially the first section out of Coffs Harbour as you climb over the range, but overall the distance should be covered fairly easily.

Leave Coffs Harbour in the direction of Coramba, by cycling down High St. (the main road), which not long after crossing the highway becomes Coramba Rd., a scenic alternative to the Pacific Highway. A few km out of town you are faced with a fairly considerable climb over the range before a fairly tame descent down to the Orara River valley, retaining most of the altitude you have just gained. There are a few smaller hills to tackle before you come to the small settlement of Coramba, about 19 km from Coffs Harbour.

Continuing on, the route flattens out somewhat as the road winds its way along the valley, bringing you to Nana Glen at the 29 km mark. There's not much here, but the small store is usually open, allowing you to purchase a refreshing, icy cold drink, something you'll appreciate if the weather is as hot for you as it was for me. The road continues to roll along, with only a limited amount of traffic to detract from your enjoyment of your pleasant surroundings. Reaching

Glenreagh after 40 km, you can have a break, and if so inclined, inquire about the tourist train to Dorrigo.

From Glenreagh, there are no major climbs, although cycling can become frustrating at times, as time and time again you negotiate a small rise followed by a brief, unsatisfying descent, regaining the same altitude many times throughout the course of the day. You cross the Orara River at Hayards Crossing after 54 km, and eventually join the Nymboida road 25 km later, turning right in the direction of Grafton. The road for the remaining distance into town is pretty much flat.

Grafton is an attractive town located on the Clarence River, famous for its tropical tree-lined streets and graceful old buildings. Every year in late October, when the trees are in magnificent mauve bloom, the town holds a jacaranda festival. While in town, a boat trip on the river is an enjoyable way to spend an hour or two. There's a good selection of accommodation available in numerous pubs, motels, and caravan parks.

Day 11   *Grafton to Casino*
(102 km/63 miles)

Although a fairly long ride, today's stretch along the Summerland Way to Casino should not prove overly taxing, especially if you beat the heat and get off to an early start. As it can get pretty hot during summer, I suggest that you stock up with water before leaving Grafton, as the only place for resupply along the way is the small settlement of Whiporie, 50 km into the ride.

Most of the route passes through low, rolling countryside with a few small climbs, peaking as you cross the summit of the Stirling range just before Whiporie, which at 50 km represents the approximate halfway point for the day. Indulge yourself in some refreshment at the store before tackling the second leg. There's a picnic area at Braemar State Forest 74 km into the ride, with tables, toilets, and a water tank where you can top your supply if necessary.

Casino (no, it doesn't have one) is a supply center for the beef, dairy, and timber industries of the surrounding district. It is located on the Bruxner Highway and also lies on the main northern rail line. Accommodation consists of a couple of pubs and caravan parks. The Royal hotel also has some newly decorated motel-style units that are comfortable and quite a good value. For a meal, check out the pubs or wander over to the RSL club, housed in a surprisingly large and modern building. Once you're signed in as a guest, avail yourself of the bar facilities and restock your energy supplies at the reasonably priced, all-you-can-eat buffet.

Day 12   *Casino to Nimbin*
half-day (50 km/31 miles)

Although today's ride is fairly short, on arriving in Nimbin you'll think you've traveled a million miles. It's Australia's alternate-lifestyle, hippy capital, and whether you love it or hate it, you'll have to admit that it's certainly unlike any other country town.

Leave Casino by getting onto the road that heads toward Bentley. You'll have to head east past the RSL club and eventually cross some railway lines. It's a quiet road passing predominantly through fairly flat farming country, although there are a couple of small but tiring climbs not far out of town. After about 14 km you come to a T-junction where you turn right to join the busier Lismore-Kyogle road.

Stay on this busier road for about 10 km, keeping an eye out for maniac truck drivers, before turning left toward Nimbin. The turnoff comes with Lismore visible in the distance, not long after crossing some railway lines. The road forks a short distance later, but you continue straight ahead (right fork) following the road signs to your destination. Not far out of Nimbin, an interesting rock formation and Aboriginal sacred site called Nimbin Rocks can be seen away to your left.

Cycling up Nimbin's main street, it doesn't take you long to realize that this town is different. All the shops sport psychedelic paint jobs, matching the garb of the colorful locals seated outside. This is where the whole hippy migration to northern NSW began, when in 1973 the town staged the Aquarius festival. There are still several communes located in the surrounding area. While in town you might want to have a look at the Marijuana Museum, where an extraordinary number of bizarre exhibits are crammed into a tiny space. More than likely you'll be offered the real thing out on the street.

For a small town, there's quite a good range of accommodation available, including a motel, pub, and two hostels. The YHA hostel is quite a nice one, with a good swimming pool and pleasant gardens. To get to it, just continue down the main street until you come to a bridge. The hostel is just down a short track away to your left. You can take a tour from the hostel to explore the rain forest of nearby Nightcap National Park, a permaculture center, Mt. Warning, or a host of other attractions in the area.

Day 13   *Nimbin to Murwillumbah*
half-day (50 km/31 miles)

Head out of town by cycling to the end of the main street, crossing over the little stream down near the youth hostel. The lightly trafficked road rolls along through lush-looking farmland, gaining on the whole more altitude than it yields, coming to a summit at Blue Knob, about 10 km into the ride. Once over Blue Knob, the craggy profiles of the peaks in the chain called the Scenic Rim become visible, including 1,156 m Mt. Warning, an extinct volcano that dominates the landscape of the far north NSW region. It was named by Captain Cook as a landmark to avoid Pt. Danger off Tweed Heads. Not far beyond Blue Knob, after 13 km you emerge on to the busier but still fairly quiet Kyogle-Murwillumbah road, turning right in the direction of your destination.

You pass first through Kunghur (just a few houses) after 23 km and Uki about 12 km later, the rolling road paralleling the Tweed River much of the way. Not far out of Uki, you come to the turnoff to Mt. Warning on the left side of the road. Although getting to the top of the road involves a tough 6 km slog uphill, if you're feeling energetic I'd thoroughly recommend it. Once at the top, there are lush palms and rain forest to explore, a walking track (4-hour walk) leading the remaining distance to the summit. If you're up there at dawn you'll be the first person in Australia to see the sun rise.

Coming into town, you encounter your first fields of sugar cane, which along with bananas constitute the principal crops of the area. The last couple of km of the ride makes the transition from rural to suburban surroundings, as you finally emerge after 50 km onto the Pacific Highway in the town center of Murwillumbah.

Murwillumbah (pop. 7,800) is the last sizeable town on the Pacific Highway before the Gold Coast. There's a wide range of accommodation available, including a YHA hostel set on a hillside overlooking the broad Tweed River. It's easy to find: jhead on down the highway and take the last left

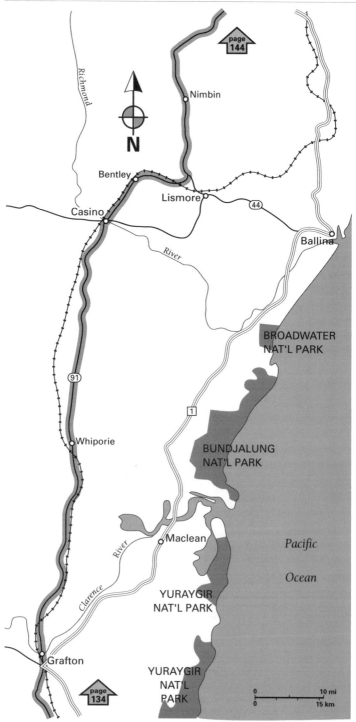

before the bridge, following the road that parallels the river for a couple of hundred meters.

Day 14   *Murwillumbah to Nerang/Gold Coast*
(70 km/43 miles to Nerang; 80 km/50 miles to Gold Coast)

Cycle down Murwillumbah's main street, Commercial St., and turn right near the post office onto a road signed to Nerang. It's not long before you're once again clear of town, crossing a small bridge over the Rous River before coming to an intersection at the 2.5 km mark, where you turn left. Just off to the right there's a magnificent grand old house in beautiful condition, decorated with lots of delicate wrought iron.

You are surrounded by sugar cane on both sides of the road as you cycle along the flat floor of the Tweed Valley, although views over to approaching hills indicate there's some climbing ahead. After 8 km you follow the road as it sort of loops around on itself, continuing in the direction of Nerang, arriving in the small village of Chillingham at the 17 km point. Near Chillingham, the terrain begins to get noticeably hillier as you begin to climb out of the valley, culminating in a tough and at times steep 3 km ascent up to the NSW/Queensland border. The view improves as you continue to gain altitude, thankfully removing some of the focus away from your burning legs. The border is marked by a crossing point where for the purpose of agricultural disease control you are obliged to part with any fruit you may be carrying. Formalities aside, it's time to take a photo next to the "Welcome to Queensland" sign and bid a fond farewell to NSW.

Your first couple of km in Queensland are downhill, making for a favorable introduction to the Sunshine State. After a km or two you pass the turnoff to the Natural Arch National Park, one of five small parks in the Springbrook area. It's not too far off the road and would make a good place to stop and have a break or even a hike if you're feeling energetic. The freewheeling descent continues until roughly the 33.5 km mark, where the road levels out at the valley floor after a small creek crossing. Not far down the road, next to the Nerang River is a picnic area with shelter and drinking water. Away to the left are some spectacular cliffs, where after rain you can see a number of waterfalls cascading down the rock face.

The road is fairly flat as you skirt along the valley floor, passing through lush-looking pastures filled with grazing dairy cattle. As the km pass, however, you begin to encounter some small hills that increase in size near the Hinze Dam. After approximately 60 km, you come to a fork in the road, where you bear left in the direction of Nerang and Binna Burra (gateway to Lamington National Park). A short time later, you catch your first glimpse of the highrise development on the Gold Coast in the distance away to your right. Traffic begins to increase during the final few km into the town of Nerang, which you reach after cycling 70 km for the day.

You could stay in Nerang, but I would recommend that you press on and head for Southport, the original town on the Gold Coast. The Gold Coast is a 35 km strip of beaches, a thoroughly commercialized resort flanked by acres of highrise development. It's not for everyone, but nevertheless is definitely worth a look or an extended stay if you find it to your liking. From Nerang, just follow the Southport road, which although very busy has quite a good shoulder for most of its 10 km length, as it passes through a rather dreary combination of light industrial and commercial areas. Finally, after 80 km or so you arrive at the coast and Southport.

There is a multitude of accommodation options to suit all price brackets on the Gold Coast. A good budget pick in Southport is Trekkers guest house at 22 White St., a clean, friendly hostel located in an old renovated house. I should also mention that at the time of writing, a rail link between Brisbane and the Gold Coast is under construction, making it easy should you feel the desire to end your tour here and train it into the capital.

Day 15   Gold Coast to Beenleigh (Brisbane)
(75 km/46.5 miles)

The final day of the tour sees you scaling picturesque Tamborine Mountain, before descending to Beenleigh, a town on the outskirts of Brisbane and situated at the end of the suburban rail network. From Beenleigh, jump on a train and sit back and relax as you escape suburban traffic, and conclude the tour by arriving in Brisbane.

From the Gold Coast, cycle north, parallel with the ocean, through Southport and Labrador for approximately 10 km (from Southport) before following the road as it heads inland toward the Pacific Highway, Coomera, and Oxenford. You pass a number of golf courses and up-market housing developments before crossing a bridge over the highway into Oxenford at about the 18 km mark. The Warner Brothers theme park "Movie World," one of a number in the area, is located only a km or so to the south, on the Pacific Highway.

Just beyond Upper Coomera, you encounter a rather steep, straight 1 km climb, before descending an equal distance immediately after reaching the summit. The quiet road is relatively flat as you skirt along the valley floor, but it gradually begins to rise as you approach the 30 km point. From here the serious climbing begins, with no respite for approximately 8 km. A local told me that from the mountain road there are outstanding views back toward the Gold Coast. I'll have to take his word for it, as my experience was one of torrential rain with low clouds making it difficult to see the road ahead, let alone the coast. You're most of the way up the hill when you pass a sign welcoming you to Eagle Heights, the road leveling out a couple of km later as you pass several Devonshire tea–style establishments.

Tamborine Mountain (alt. 560 m, 1,824 ft.), a popular weekend getaway for Brisbane locals, boasts not one but nine small national parks, which are home to subtropical rain forests, waterfalls, and a number of native animals including the rarely seen platypus. If you've got some time, take a break from the bike, have lunch, and explore some of the art and craft shops or one of the many walking trails in the area. Should you wish to stay longer, there are a number of places offering accommodation on the mountain.

Eventually the road comes to a roundabout, where you turn right on the Eagle Heights road, in the direction of North Tamborine and Beaudesert, coming to another T-junction at Curtis Falls a short distance later. Turn right here, signed to Brisbane via Tamborine. Your effort in climbing up the mountain is justly rewarded by a lengthy, exhilarating 8 km descent down a road with numerous switchbacks and hairpin bends. The road is still slightly downhill as you come to the outskirts of Tamborine at the 52 km point, where you turn right down a road signed to Beenleigh.

This is the home stretch, with only 23 km of good- quality, rolling road separating you from the finishing point of a quite lengthy tour. The distance passes quickly, the anticipation of finishing the tour more than compensating for flagging

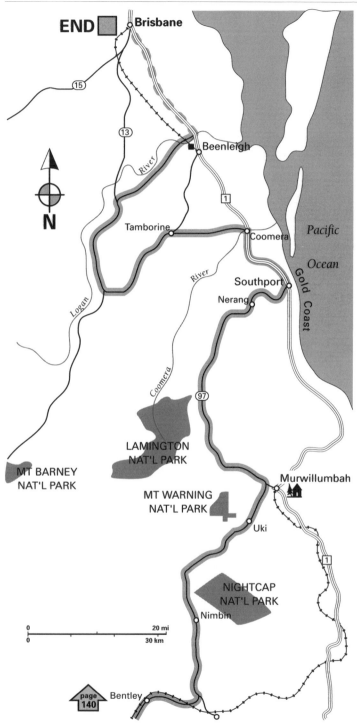

energy reserves. There are a couple of km of ever- expanding suburbs to cycle through before you arrive in the town of Beenleigh proper, once a center in its own right but now really an outer suburb of Brisbane. Once you've located the train station, which is near the center of town, board one of the frequent trains for the final leg of your journey into Brisbane. You must pay for your bike and carry it in the first carriage of the train, closest to the engine. Relax, enjoy the train trip, and congratulate yourself on completing a lengthy but varied tour.

Brisbane

Only a few years ago, both Brisbanites and visitors alike used to say that Brisbane felt like a big country town. That is much less the case these days, as the city has undergone something of a building boom in the last ten years, and many businessmen and politicians are keen to replace the country town image with that of the modern business center.

It is Australia's third-largest city with a population of 1.7 million. It started life as yet another penal settlement; however, that petered out in 1839, and thereafter it was populated by free settlers. It is a fine city situated on the Brisbane River, with some attractive parks, buildings and squares, and views to surrounding hills. Although the city is developing and modernizing, you will still see the old tropical Queensland stilt house in many of the suburbs.

Among the fine old buildings are the old observatory and windmill (1829), Old Government House (1862) and Old St. Stephens, the city's oldest church (1850). There are several more buildings of historical interest; you can get more details from the tourist office in the City Hall. Brisbane also has several museums and galleries worth a visit, a lush and exotic botanic gardens, the very pleasant King George Square, and some thriving shopping malls, in particular the Queen St. mall, which is the hub of central city shopping.

If you are not having a rest from cycling there's a nice ride of about 7 km along the river from the botanic gardens to the University of Queensland. Getting around by other means is also pretty easy, as there's a comprehensive city bus service and a suburban rail network.

There are two YHA hostels, the Brisbane City hostel in Quay St. and the Brisbane Gardens in Mitchell St. Kedron. There are also quite a few backpacker hostels, particularly in

Fortitude Valley and Paddington, as well as near the Roma St. transport terminal. You will find no shortage of budget eating places, and as in other large Australian cities, there's a great diversity of ethnic cuisines.

Chapter 11.
Perth to Albany

This tour takes you through Western Australia's beautiful southwest, which is particularly delightful in spring when the wildflowers are in bloom. In parts it is a challenging ride, with some long stretches between stopovers. At the same time, it is very rewarding, taking you from the Perth coastal plane, through farming country and jarrah forest to the Blackwood River, the spectacular giant karri forests of the Pemberton region and Walpole area, and finally along a pretty stretch of coast from Denmark to historic Albany.

Start	Perth City
Finish	Albany
Distance	641 km (400 miles)
Duration	12 days (9 cycling days)
Road Conditions	Quiet to very quiet roads, mostly well surfaced and in good condition. Dirt road for 74 km from just south of Dwellingup to north of Collie and for 19 km from Noggerup toward Balingup. The Dwellingup-to-Collie section is tough in parts, with areas of soft surface and hills. No real difficulties on the Noggerup section.
	If you don't wish to tackle the gravel road from Dwellingup to Collie, or if you don't have enough time to complete the full tour, you may wish to start from Collie, which you can reach from Perth on a Westrail bus.
Terrain	Mainly flat in the Perth coastal plain and along the south coast, with undulating road and gentle to moderate hills in between.

Climate   Temperate, though can be hot in summer. There
is often a southwesterly to southeasterly wind.

Accomm.   There are YHA, other backpackers, country
hotels, motels, caravan parks, camping grounds,
B&B, rented cabins/cottages, farm stays.

Route Description

Day 1   **Perth to Serpentine**
(63 km/39 miles)

This first part of the tour takes you out of central Perth on a 30
km cycle track alongside the Swan River and the Kwinana
Freeway, until you are well south of the city. You then travel
on quiet back roads through flat farmland to the small
settlement of Serpentine, close to the Darling ranges.

If you are feeling energetic you may wish to carry on to
Dwellingup in a single day. Dwellingup is a pretty little town
set in the jarrah forest 110 km from Perth. Bear in mind,
however, that the next stage of the ride from Dwellingup to
Collie on the gravel road through the forest is 97 km and
quite tiring, so unless you plan to rest for a day in
Dwellingup, you may prefer to take two days to get there.

From Perth you take the cycleway south along the river
and the Kwinana Freeway. To locate the start of the cycle
path, go to the No. 2 car park off Mounts Bay Rd. opposite the
intersection with Mill St. At the back of the car park, you will
see the cycle path, which passes under a flyover bridge,
crosses a one-way road, and then takes you through an
underpass. Follow the path and cross the Narrows bridge,
curving left under the bridge on the southern side and
following the cycle path, with the freeway on your left and
the river on your right. This is just one of the many great
cycleways to be found round the river system of Perth. If you
are in this beautiful city for any length of time and want to
explore more riverside rides, get hold of a little free
publication put out by Bikewest (ph (09) 430 7550) called
"Around the Rivers Ride—Recreation Cycle Tour."

After approximately 5 km you come to Canning bridge, a
low wooden bridge adjacent to the Raffles hotel. Pass under
the bridge and follow the cyclepath to Mt. Henry bridge.
Cross the bridge and proceed straight along a laneway, which
has the bridge and freeway on the left and garden fencing on

the right. After about 75 m, you cross a road and ride along a quiet suburban road (signed "cycle path to Leach Highway") parallel with the freeway for about 500 m.

You will see a busy highway on your left (Leach Highway), which you cross at a crossing point with traffic lights. You turn right, and about 50 m later the cycleway resumes on your left. From here to the end of the Kwinana Freeway you simply follow the cycle path, keeping the freeway on your left. The path is new and has an excellent fine surface. There must be few cities indeed where cyclists can travel through 30 km of suburbs in such safety and with such ease.

The Kwinana Freeway ends at the 31 km mark. Turn right into Thomas Rd., and 100 m later turn left into Johnson Rd. Proceed down Johnson Rd. for 3.5 km until you come to a T-junction with a railway. Turn right, then after 800 m turn left into Wellard Rd. About 250 m later you cross the railway and turn right into Millar Rd. Almost immediately, you turn left into Baldivis Rd.

Baldivis Rd. is a fairly quiet bitumen lane, which runs through flattish farmland past small holdings and horse stables. In the cooler times of the year it is quite green and pretty. In the heat of summer it is brown and scorched. At just over 46 km from Perth, you will see Serpentine signed 16 km down Serpentine Rd. Ignore this and proceed a further 2 km to Karnup Rd., where Serpentine is signed 15 km to the left.

You ride along a quiet back road through flat pasture. At 51 km, you turn right over a river and then just keep following Karnup Rd. until you reach Serpentine at 63 km. The town center is actually a couple of km further on. It is a small quiet place with a pub, a few houses, and a general store/supermarket. The pub sells good counter meals at lunchtime and in the early evening.

If you do plan to stay here, the accommodation is basically limited to either caravan accommodation or camping at the Serpentine Falls leisure village at the corner of Falls Rd. and the South West Highway. At the time of writing the caravans are $45 for two, with limited pillows/linen available for hire. The camping ground is $18 for two, $10 for one, which includes power.

The Serpentine Falls are a pleasant local beauty spot, as is the Serpentine dam in the nearby hills.

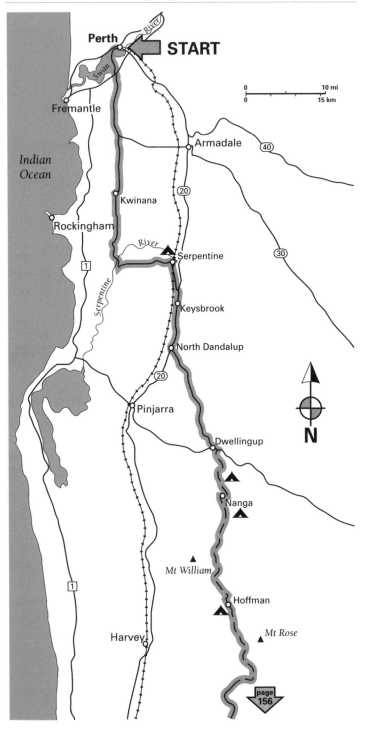

Day 2   **Serpentine to Dwellingup**
             (42.5 km/26.5 miles)

This ride is basically in two parts. For the first 18 km or so you travel on a flat road through pretty farmland with the Darling ranges on your left. Over the last 25 km, you climb into the hills and travel through attractive jarrah forest and bushland.

To avoid the South West Highway, which can sometimes be busy, ride back into the town of Serpentine, turn right by the railway line, and ride parallel with the railway line for 200 m or so until you come to the level crossing and roundabout. Turn left into Halls Rd. on the other side of the railway line and follow this for about 6 km until it curves left across the railway line into Fisher Rd. About 700 m later, you join the South West Highway and turn right.

This is not a bad road to ride on, as there is a space a meter or so wide to the left of the traffic lane, which keeps you separate from the traffic on a good surface. The scenery is very pleasant, with green pastures and gentle hills to the left. At about 10.5 km you pass the Keysbrook general store if you need refreshment. Eight km further on, you come to North Dandalup, a small settlement along the highway, with a pub, a few houses, and a service station that also sells fast food meals and snacks.

You turn left to Dwellingup at the side of the Black and Gold service station. It is 25 km from this point. The road climbs a very gentle gradient, which becomes steeper about 2.5 km from the Black and Gold store. From here to Dwellingup, you climb a great deal and also enjoy a few descents, but none of the hills are too tough. The country is very pretty jarrah forest and native bushland, with a few green hills in between.

At various intervals you will see wooden signs indicating that much of this forest is part of a regrowth program. Some of it was replanted 40–50 years ago, while other sections are as young as 10 years old. On the day I traveled this stretch, there were plenty of birds in full voice—colorful rosellas and green "twenty-eight" parrots. The road was quiet, and yellow acacias were in full bloom. This is why cycle touring can be so brilliant: you just don't get to be part of the scene like this in a car.

Just over 34 km from Serpentine, a long conveyor belt that disappears each way into the distance passes underneath the road. This is bringing bauxite from the Darling ranges to an aluminum refinery in the town of Pinjarra. At 42 km you enter the outskirts of Dwellingup, and 2 km further on you are in the town center. Dwellingup is a small town set in the forest, which achieved notoriety in 1961 because of a devastating fire. It is a good location for forest and bush walks, and there are a number of campsites close to the town. Nanga Mill, 10 km from the town center, is the only campsite with fresh water, but this must be boiled before drinking. There is bunkhouse-style accommodation at Dwellingup cabins in River Rd. (linen required), or you can stay at the Dwellingup community hotel for around $28 per night.

Day 3   Dwellingup to Collie
(95.7 km/58.4 miles)

This day's ride takes you on a predominantly gravel surface through the forest to the southwest town of Collie. You will need to take plenty of water, as there are no sources of fresh water beyond Nanga (water must be boiled) just south of Dwellingup. Although it is quite a challenging ride, given that you will be riding on gravel for most of the day, it is a great experience. The forest environment is scenic and restful, you will encounter very few cars, and you may well see wildlife that includes wallabies, kangaroos, emus, and a host of parrots and other forest birds.

The gravel surface is actually quite reasonable once you get used to it, though it is naturally more taxing on the slight hills that you encounter from time to time. This ride is best if you set out early and give yourself plenty of time to make a few stops and enjoy the peacefulness of the forest. Mountain bikes will fare much better than tourers in these conditions.

Leaving Dwellingup town center, turn left into River Rd.; then, just over a km further on, turn right into Nanga Rd., signed 89 km to Collie. The road winds down a scenic road through partly cleared forest to a bridge over the Murray River, where the sealed road ends soon afterwards. You will be riding through the forest on gravel for the next 74 km. The road varies between flat stretches and undulating rises and descents. Be careful when riding on this surface—if you let yourself ride too fast you can lose control and easily come off.

At 13 km you pass Nanga picnic area and campsite. This was the site of a jarrah sawmill that was burnt down in the great fire of 1961. There are toilets, picnic tables, and fireplaces beneath the trees, with plenty of wood for fires.

There is also tap water, which must be boiled before drinking. At 28.4 km there is a fork in the road, with zigzag road bearing to the right. You take the left fork and continue on an undulating road. It was not far from here that we saw an emu scuttle through the trees at considerable speed, and a little further on a wallaby hopped noisily through the undergrowth. At 41.8 km you come to another picnic spot at Hoffman's Pool. It has a chemical toilet, some tables and benches, but no fresh water. We stopped for a break and enjoyed our lunch against the backdrop of a chorus of parrots flitting from tree to tree.

At 55 km take care to ensure that you turn left down the Tallanalla road to Collie. This may not strike you as obvious at first, as the road you are on carries on straight ahead. About 2.5 km down the Tallanalla road from this point, you cross a bridge over a conveyor belt carrying bauxite from a site in the Darling ranges to the aluminum refinery at Worsley. From here to the recommencement of the sealed road at 81.7 km, the road undulates through the forest, though there are a couple of long, slow climbs that are quite taxing on the leg muscles because of the gravel surface.

Just before the sealed road recommences, the scenery changes, with the dense forest giving way to cleared land and young plantation pines. About 500 m after you hit the sealed road, there is a T-junction at which you turn right. For the next 12 km into Collie you follow a fairly quiet undulating road through farmland. The center of Collie is about 2 km from the sign on the outskirts.

Collie (pop. 7,667) is a pleasant-looking town whose main reason for existence is coal mining, though this fact is not immediately obvious. There are no mines visible, no grime or soot or any of the other things that you sometimes associate with a coal mining town. The mines, both underground and open-cut, are outside the town itself.

There is some attractive country to enjoy near Collie, or if you wish you can visit a tourist coal mine or the Coalfields Museum. In terms of accommodation there are a number of older-style hotels offering bed and breakfast at around $27–35 per person, with the Collie motel rather more expensive. There is also the Mt. Marron holiday village in Porter St., where on-site caravans cost around $25 for two, with each extra person $5. There are a small number of restaurants in Collie, and the pubs serve counter meals.

Day 4   Collie to Nannup
(101 km/63 miles)

This part of the tour takes you through more pleasant farmland and forest country on quiet roads and includes a 19 km stretch on gravel, just outside Noggerup. From Balingup you enjoy a delightful road, which follows Balingup Brook and the Blackwood River to Nannup. With some justification, this stretch of road is described in much of the tourist literature as being of outstanding natural beauty.

With the exception of Balingup, there is no opportunity to buy refreshment or supplies until you reach Nannup.

From the Collie motel in Throssell St. you turn right, ride past the shops, and then turn right near the bowling club, signed 21 km to Mumballup and 66 km to Boyup Brook. The road takes you out of Collie over the river, past small industrial workshops on the outskirts of town. You are soon mainly climbing through a mix of open forest and farming country on a quiet road with a good surface. Our progress was somewhat slowed by a stiff southeasterly breeze. Throughout the southwest of Western Australia you will find a prevailing southwesterly to southeasterly wind.

At 21 km you arrive at a T-junction, with the Mumballup tavern standing in splendid isolation 100 m to the right. This is virtually all the evidence of human settlement that you see at Mumballup, though I guess there are also a couple of scattered farms in the area. It was early in the morning when we stopped outside the tavern, so it wasn't open. However, it does claim to serve counter meals. It was an odd, peaceful spot—there wasn't a soul around except us. The bus that plies between Perth and various towns in the southwest stops outside the Mumballup tavern; I'm not sure who for.

Back to the route, you turn left at the Mumballup T-junction (i.e., you don't go past the tavern) and head toward Noggerup. For the next 7 km to Noggerup, you cycle through pleasant open grazing country on a straight, flat road. There is a little more traffic on this section, but you can still describe it as fairly light.

At Noggerup (again no sign of any settlement to speak of) you turn right on a road signed Balingup 32 km, Grimwade 19 km. After a couple of hundred meters, the sealed road peters out, and you find yourself riding on a fairly soft gravel road. You stay on the unsealed road for 19 km, traveling through some very pretty state forest. The ride is not too difficult; the road has some gentle rises and falls and is a bit slippery in places, but it is easier than parts of the Dwellingup-Collie section. There is almost zero traffic.

Just before you come to the end of this 19 km unsealed stretch, you pass through a pine plantation. You then are on the sealed Grimwade road and proceed straight ahead, climbing for the first couple of km, then descending for the next three. From this point you gradually descend to the junction with the South West Highway another 7 km away. You turn left at the junction with the South West Highway. Balingup is 1 km down the road.

Balingup is a pretty little country town whose main industries are timber, fruit growing, dairying, and sheep farming. There is a general store, a tearoom that sells sandwiches and light meals, and a number of craft shops. There are a few B&Bs, most of which cost in excess of $50 per night. There is also the Kirrup Kabins chalets (blankets and pillows supplied), which cost $70 for two, 1995 prices.

Leaving Balingup, you turn right on Brockman St. signed 41 km to Nannup. The road winds and undulates through small valleys of fields and pine plantations. Just over 12 km from Balingup, you come to Wrights bridge—a bridge over the Blackwood River with a very pleasant camping ground and picnic site close by, with fireplaces and safe swimming. At this point the Bibulmen Track walking trail cuts across your path. Just over 4 km past Wrights bridge you will see Lewana Valley cottages on your left. It is an old Ministry of Sport and Recreation property set on lush green lawns, which provides budget accommodation for families and groups. There are five 2- and 3-bedroom cottages that will accommodate up to ten people, but you have to supply your own blankets and linen. The 1995 cost of hiring the cottages was $46–55 per day. The telephone number for booking is (09) 387 9733.

The countryside here is very pretty, with native forest and the river on your right and pine plantations on the left. The road narrows after Lewana Valley cottages, but it is still very quiet and peaceful. This is one of those stretches that makes you glad you are cycle touring and not rushing along inside a car.

At 86 km you pass self-contained cottage accommodation on your left at Beyonderup Falls. There are two cottages here that accommodate 6–8 people. Call (097) 56 2034 for details. A km farther, you will see Redgum guest house on your right.

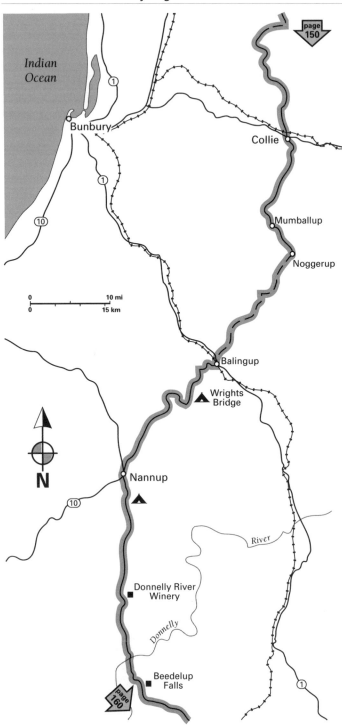

This is a more up-market B&B and costs in the vicinity of $70 for one and $110 for two.

The last 5–6 km to Nannup are quite hilly, so after a long day's riding, albeit through great country, I was glad to coast down a hill into the center of town. It was the weekend of the Nannup Folk (music) Festival and the town was full to overflowing, so we retraced our steps to the Balingup road caravan park on the outskirts of town and pitched our tent for $5 each. It's a very pleasant spot near the river, but the ground is extremely hard, so you will need good sturdy tent pegs and a hammer.

Nannup (pop. 552) is a lovely little town, first settled by Europeans between 1850 and 1862. Its main industries are timber, fruit-growing, and dairy farming. Apart from the Balingup road caravan park there is the Nannup caravan park close to the center of town, the Black Cockatoo hostel (which accommodates fourteen people at $10 per night), a number of holiday cottages and B&Bs at varying prices, and the Nannup motel-hotel. The tourist information center is on Brockman St. There are a couple of cafe/restaurants, and the hotel serves counter meals.

If you decide to stay over in Nannup, activities include hiring a canoe, taking one of a number of river trips and tours, visiting a saw mill, or taking one of the Nannup Heritage Trail walks (either 2.5 km or 9 km). There are also galleries, craft shops, and a couple of small museums.

Day 5. Nannup to Pemberton
(78 km/48 miles)

This part of the tour takes you through a very pleasant mixture of hilly green farmland and native forest. As you near Pemberton you will enjoy the exhilarating experience of cycling through the giant karri trees. The road is quiet and has a good-quality surface. You should note that there are no shops or other outlets where you can purchase a drink until you reach the Karri Valley resort 57.5 km from Nannup, so make sure that you have adequate water and food with you.

From the Nannup hotel you ride through the town in the direction of the Pemberton road. At 2.5 km from the hotel you turn left, signed 74 km to Pemberton. The road is fringed with trees on each side and runs through pleasant green agricultural land. At 7 km you experience a long winding descent and continue for 12 km or so through the same hilly farmland interspersed with pockets of trees. At 19 km the farmland gives way to forest for 7 km or so. This pattern of pretty farmland interspersed with pockets of forest is characteristic of this road most of the way to Pemberton.

At 30 km we came across a roadside fruit stall on the left near a house. You buy your fruit on the honor system, leaving your money in a tin. At 37 km the road narrows somewhat and the terrain becomes a little hillier. At 42 km you make a nice gradual descent to the Donnelly River winery, then undertake a slow climb of about 800 m up the other side of the valley.

The road continues between the trees, and at 51.5 km there is a very pleasant 2 km descent. From about the 56 km mark the trees become noticeably larger and the forest becomes thicker on both sides of the road. These are the famous giant karri trees that are characteristic of the Pemberton area. At 57.5 km you see the Karri Valley resort on the right. There is a shop here, your first opportunity since leaving Nannup to buy food and drink. Karri Valley resort is a popular holiday spot with varying types of accommodation.

Just past the Karri Valley resort the trees are taller still, and it is an awesome experience to be cycling through such a magnificent stretch of forest. At 62 km the countryside opens out a little, and you find yourself in pleasant farmland again. Over the next couple of km there are some quite steep rises and falls as the road curves round the contours of small valleys. The road passes in and out of pockets of forest, and at 73.7 km, when you emerge from the forest, you will see holiday cabins on your right. At 75 km you can look down on Pemberton in the valley on your left. At 76 km you come to a T- junction where you turn left and roll down a 2 km hill into Pemberton.

There is a good range of accommodation in Pemberton. At the budget end of the scale, the Warren Lodge backpacker's is a good value at $12 per night. The rooms are all lockable, and are mainly twin with a couple of doubles. There is a good kitchen/lounge area with TV and a few board games. The same establishment also does budget bed and breakfast. The YHA is 10 km northwest of the town in a lovely setting in the forest and costs $10 per night. There are motels, a caravan park, and also lots of chalets/cottages for rent, which tend to be a better value if there are 3 or 4 of you staying. There are also plenty of B&B from moderate to boutique/expensive. The tourist information center is halfway up Brockman St., and there is plenty of information on hand about accommodation and things to do. There are forest walks, a winery where you can sample the wine, a tram ride to Northcliffe 30 km through the forest—and you must visit the Gloucester Tree, a huge karri, which you can climb at your own risk via a metal ladder hammered into the side of the trunk.

There is a reasonable array of places to eat. The Pemberton hotel does very good counter meals. There are also motel dining rooms, a fried chicken take-away, and 3 or 4 small restaurants.

Pemberton is a lovely little town in the karri forest; it is well worth stopping over for a day or two on your way through to Albany.

Day 6   Pemberton to Northcliffe
(30 km/19 miles)

This is a comparatively short but very attractive ride on a virtually traffic-free road through some beautiful tall forest. As Northcliffe is a quiet little town, you may wish to spend extra time in Pemberton and arrive in Northcliffe toward the end of the day.

Leaving Pemberton from the Warren Lodge in Brockman St., you turn right, go down the hill for 800 m, and then ascend quite steeply for 1.5 km until you reach the turnoff to Nannup at the top of the hill. You continue straight ahead to Northcliffe, signed 27 km shortly after the T-junction. At just over the 5 km mark there is a turnoff on the left to the Cascades scenic tourist drive. The road descends through slightly thicker forest on the left and then flattens out a couple of km later after a turnoff to Warren on the right. You then wind up and down through some lovely tall trees, which looked especially fine in the early morning with the sun coming through. For the next several km the undulating road winds around curves through alternating stretches of tall and then smaller native trees. There is almost no traffic, just a lovely quiet punctuated by bird sounds.

At 22.5 km you cross the Pemberton-to-Northcliffe tramway line after riding down a long, gradual hill. Soon you are traveling through farmland again, and at 29 km you pass the "Welcome to Northcliffe" sign. The road curves round a left-hand bend and the small town of Northcliffe appears—a service station, a supermarket, and a few shops on the left, a

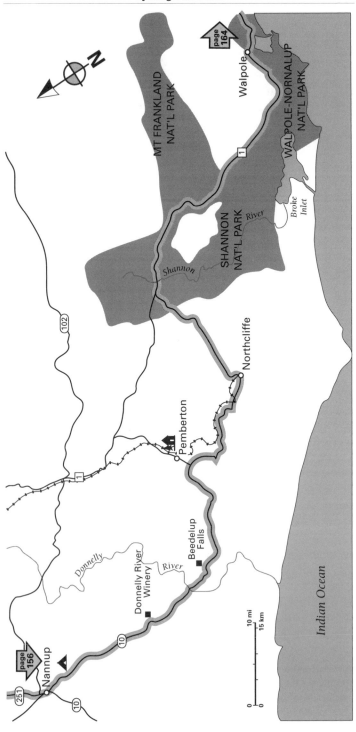

pioneer museum and tourist information center ahead and slightly to the right at the crossroads.

Northcliffe is a quiet little town of 208 people situated in the forest. It promotes itself as the gateway to a south coast recreational area that includes Windy Harbour 29 km away on the coast, and Point D'Entrecasteaux, where 150 m cliffs rise above the ocean. Taken as a whole, this area offers pursuits such as bush walking, boating, and fishing.

There is a small range of accommodation, and the tourist information center has a useful list with prices. The Northcliffe hotel is $16 single, $30 double, and $7 for breakfast; an on-site van at the caravan park is $25, and the Meerup Springs self-contained cabins are $60 per couple and $10 for each extra person. The campsite at Windy Harbour is $3 per person per night, but only offers cold showers. Choice of eating places is limited—the Northcliffe hotel serves counter meals and there is Witchetty's restaurant, which serves breakfast, sandwiches, light meals, and main meals.

Day 7   Northcliffe to Walpole
(98.6 km/61 miles)

This part of the tour takes you predominantly through forest including more tall karri. Nearer to Walpole there are stretches where the trees are smaller and not particularly attractive, but there is also the magnificent red tingle tree which grows only in the Walpole area. There are some hilly stretches where the going is quite slow—it took me almost 7 hours. Over the whole route there are no places where you can buy a drink until you reach Walpole, so make sure you take some food and fill up your water bottles.

From the Northcliffe hotel you head left on the Walpole/Albany road. This quiet road undulates through attractive trees at the roadside with views of farmland beyond the trees on the right. At approximately 2.5 km you turn right onto Middleton Rd., signed to Walpole and Albany, and for the next few km you ride along a flat, good-quality road through more grassy farmland, punctuated by pockets of forest. At 7.6 km a wooden sign tells you that you are in the Jane State Forest.

After 11 km the road dips down and takes you on a straight course for 7 km through some spectacular tall trees. After passing through mixed forest and farmland, you see another roadside sign at 23.5 km, which indicates that you are in the Shannon National Park. Just over 5 km later you come to a T-junction with the South West Highway and turn right, following the sign to Walpole and Albany. A few hundred meters later, a green direction board indicates that Walpole is 69 km.

For the next few km you experience a mixture of tall and then smaller native trees, and at just over 32 km you reach Shannon, where you will see a camping area signed. (There appears to be nothing at all there except for the sign.) The road winds and undulates through stretches of pretty forest, and at just over 40 km from Northcliffe you enter the Mt. Frankland National Park. A couple of km later you are in the Weld State Forest, where huge trees stand right on the road's edge. Further down the road, where you pass a sign indicating 45 km to Walpole, the trees become smaller and scrubbier and rather unattractive. This landscape would probably best be described as coastal scrub. At 73.6 km there is a sign on the right to Broke Inlet and at 79 km, just after a road sign to Center Crossing, the trees become taller and more attractive again.

At 86 km you come to Crystal Springs, where a few fields with grazing cattle appear; there is a camping ground. Just over 3 km later you descend to the Deep River Bridge, climb up the other side and pass a sign announcing the Walpole/Nornalup National Park. After a slow climb the road levels out, and at 93.3 km you pass a sign on the right to Tinglewood. From here the trees are taller and more attractive—the ones with the reddish trunks are tingle trees. Seven hundred meters further on is the John Rate lookout, where you can look down on the ocean inlet at Walpole. From here, the last 5 km into the town is mainly downhill. You pass the sign announcing Walpole at 98.6 km and enter the town by rounding a corner where the hotel is situated. There is a line of shops on the right, which includes a supermarket, a service station, craft shops, a bank, and a couple of cafes. Opposite the shops is a small caravan park and the tourist information office.

Walpole is a small, quiet town (pop. 291), situated on the banks of an inlet, surrounded by red tingle and karri forests. There is bush walking, fishing, and canoeing, and you can take a trip on a boat round the inlet. For accommodation there is a hotel/motel, a backpacker's called Tingle All Over, a caravan park, cabins, self-contained units, and B&B. You can eat at the hotel or at one of the cafes.

Day 8   **Walpole to Denmark via Valley of the Giants**
              (74.5 km/46 miles)

This part of the tour takes you close to the south coast and through the tingle forest and the Valley of the Giants. The ride ends in the delightful little town of Denmark, situated on the Denmark River and the Wilson Inlet. On the way, there are opportunities to buy refreshments at Nornalup, Bow Bridge, and the Wynella tearooms.

From the Tingle All Over backpacker's you turn right and head slightly downhill toward Denmark. At 2 km there are signs both left and right to scenic drives, and from here the road climbs and winds for a few hundred meters before leveling out and passing between trees. The landscape soon changes to more of a bushy coastal vegetation, and the road continues to twist and undulate. At 8.7 km you cross the Frankland River and enter the little settlement of Nornalup, which offers trips on the Frankland River to tourists, as well as canoeing and cycling along forest tracks. After a short climb out of Nornalup you are riding through a mixture of forest and fields.

At 13.7 km you come to the sign for Valley of the Giants, which turns off 250 m to the left. I recommend that you take this detour, as it is only 8 km further than the direct route to Denmark. It is on a sealed road and is well worth the extra effort for the beautiful forest scenery. If it is of interest, the Dingo Flats YHA is 8.5 km down this road. After turning left onto the road to the Valley of the Giants, you climb gently for the first few hundred meters as the road winds round to the right through some magnificent trees. You continue riding through spectacular forest complete with bird song, until you see a sign with an arrow indicating the Valley of the Giants at 19.5 km. There is a space for cars at the side of the road, from which you walk or ride 200–300 m to a wooden information shelter, which details something of the ecology and properties of the tingle tree. You can then follow a short signed walk, which takes you past several of the giant trees, many of which have fully hollowed-out trunks. Although this area is very attractive, hundred of these beautiful giant trees were taken by the loggers over the years, with the result that you will see only a comparatively few of the real giants now.

From the Valley of the Giants you continue on the road toward Bow Bridge and Denmark. You enjoy a pleasant descent for the first 1.5 km and soon come to a cleared area of

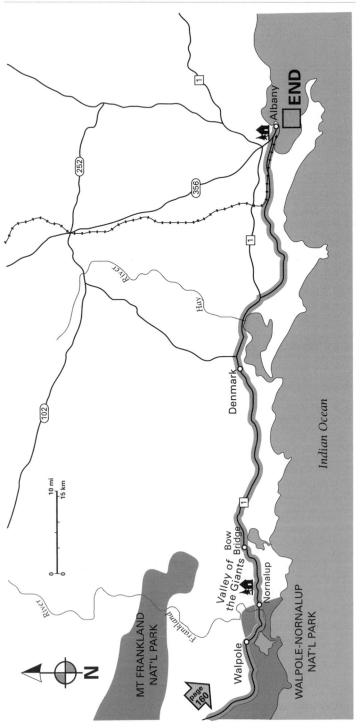

green fields and grazing cattle. At 22.6 km you see the sign for Dingo Flats youth hostel on the left. Continue on this quiet road through green farmland until you reach the Denmark-Walpole road T-junction at 31.8 km, where you turn left signed 42 km to Denmark. This is Bow Bridge, and there is a roadhouse on the left where you can grab a drink or something to eat. A couple of km further on, as you cycle through a mix of coastal scrub and farmland, you catch glimpses of the inlet on your right. This type of landscape continues for several km, and there are some long, straight stretches of road.

At 38.7 km there is a sign on the left to a woolcraft shop and an emu farm. A little further on, you pass another craft shop at the side of the road by the Kent River. This part of Western Australia, particularly the Denmark area, has attracted a sizeable number of "alternative lifestyle" settlers and craftspeople in recent years, and there is no doubt that they have added an interest and diversity to the region and to its economy.

At 45 km you can see a long, straight stretch of road laid out in front of you like a shallow roller coaster. At 48.4 km, cabins and camping are signed to the right down Boat Harbor Rd. From here the vista opens out on both sides, and you can see rocky coastal outcrops ahead and to the right. About 10 km further on, you pass signs for bed and breakfast, which reflect the fact that you are entering a very popular holiday area, and at 59.2 km you pass "Wynella Afternoon Teas" on the right, where you can buy refreshment.

A few hundred meters farther, there's a gradual curving climb for 1 km on a wider, more modern road, and at this point you get a nice view over a valley and farmland on the left. At 62 km there's a sign to an alpaca farm (more wool for the craftspeople), and for the next few km you pass through trees, which give way to farmland once more as you draw near to Denmark. Scattered along this part of the route are more signs to B&Bs, chalets, and holiday cabins. At just over 71 km you catch glimpses of the ocean on your right, and only 1.5 km later you are on the outskirts of Denmark.

Denmark is a very pretty little town of 985 people. Its name incidentally derives from Dr. Alexander Denmark, a naval physician from 1814 to 1835. The town is situated on the Denmark River on a rugged and interesting coastline. Denmark is very neat and well kept, with lush green grass down to the river's edge and some lovely native shrubs and flowers in the main shopping street. There are some interesting shops, including a couple of bakeries, an environmental shop, a bookshop, craft shops, and a gourmet food outlet. There is also a bank and a small number of restaurants. The pub overlooks the river and sells counter meals.

There is a lot of accommodation in the Denmark area, less in the town itself. In Denmark itself, the pub by the river has motel-style units; there's another hotel/motel on Inlet Dr., and a caravan park and B&B, including Edinburgh House, right in the middle of town.

Apart from boating, bush walking, fishing, and prawning, there are craft galleries and wineries to visit, and you can take an escorted trail ride on horseback through the coastal wilderness. The tourist bureau is on Strickland St. opposite the post office.

Day 9   *Denmark to Albany via Torbay Inlet* *(57.7 km/36 miles)*

This last leg of the tour takes you through farmland and coastal scenery to the historic regional center of Albany, situated round the twin peaks of Mt. Melville and Mt. Clarence on the magnificent Princess Royal Harbour. The terrain for much of this last stretch of the tour is flatter than many of the earlier sections, so you should arrive in Albany feeling comparatively fresh.

From the center of Denmark, cross the bridge over the river and head toward Albany. You will climb slightly at first, then the road flattens out as you ride past houses and the Denmark Agricultural College on your left. After 1 km there is a sign warning you of kangaroos on the road. Instead of roos I saw herds of cows grazing in a pleasant pastoral scene to the left of me.

For the next few km you experience a comparatively hilly section through farmland on the left, with occasional views of the ocean to the right, as well as signs to various beaches. The road then flattens out, and there are some long, straight stretches. It is a very quiet road with a good surface, if a bit coarse. At 17.4 km you turn right down a road signed Albany via Torbay. This even quieter road has a real country lane feel, with green fields, grazing cattle, and a few gentle hills in the distance. After a long straight stretch you come to a dot-on-the-map sort of place called Youngs Siding at 18.8 km, where there is a general store on the right. There are some further long straight stretches of road, and at 22.8 km you will see a sign to tearooms and Lownes Beach on the right. At 29 km there's a lovely view of the ocean against a rocky headland, with grazing cattle in the foreground.

At 41.7 km you come to the little settlement of Elleker, where there is a general store on the right (which sells venison). As you are winding out of Elleker you will see a railway line on your left. This follows the road the remainder of the way to Albany. From here to Albany the road is predominantly flat and very quiet, and it takes you through a landscape of mainly coastal scrub. At 47.7 km you come to a little place called Cuthbert, where there are a few cottages and some kind of small industrial plant. You are now within 10 km of Albany, and as you near the town you will pass a number of small factories and light industrial sites. Straight ahead you will see the look-out structure on the top of Mt. Melville, which is a popular tourist spot and has some great views over the town and the ocean.

At 55 km you come to a T-junction, with Frenchman's Bay and a whole series of south coast tourist spots signed to the right and Albany to the left. You turn left, cross the railway line, then turn right, signed Albany Town Center. You will see industry on the water's edge on the right, but soon you get a great view of the harbor. At 57 km you ride past the replica of a sailing ship—the *Amity* brig—on your left. Just past here at 57.7 km, you are signed left into the town center, and you are in the heart of Albany at the bottom of York St.—journey's end.

Albany is the first site in Western Australia to be settled by Europeans. Afraid that the French would colonize the area, Captain Lockyer landed on the shores of the Princess Royal Harbour from the brig *Amity* in 1826 with fifty-two convicts and their escorting soldiers. This was two years earlier than the settlement of the Swan River Colony (present-day Perth). Exploring colonists opened up the surrounding land for farming, and Albany became the commercial center for these activities. Until the turn of the century when Fremantle opened, it was also an important coaling station for mail steamers to the United Kingdom. Today, Albany is a commercial center and a major Western Australian tourist destination.

There is a lot to see and do in Albany, including swimming on the lovely Middleton Beach, and visiting historical buildings in the town and wineries in the surrounding districts. There are whale-watching boat trips at certain times of the year and also a number of boat charters and tours for activities such as snorkeling with the seals, reef snorkeling, scuba diving, and fishing, You can also enjoy spectacular views from the top of Mt. Clarence.

There is an abundance of accommodation in Albany— hotels, motels, caravan parks, a YHA and two other backpacker hostels, B&B, rented cottages, and chalets. You will also find a good choice of eating places. There are a couple of quite up-market restaurants in York St., as well as pizza places, Chinese restaurants of varying sophistication, the usual global fast food chains, counter meals, hotel dining rooms, and more.

If you are returning to Perth when you have enjoyed what Albany has to offer, you can catch the Westrail bus, which makes regular journeys between the two destinations. Bear in mind that they have a policy of transporting only two bikes on any one journey; but you could always ride your bike back.

Chapter 12.
Avon Valley Tour

This short circular tour takes you into the historic Avon Valley, the site of Western Australia's first inland European settlement in the 1830s. It is a good compact tour to do if your time in WA is limited and you want to see something of the state other than Perth and Fremantle.

The ride will take you to the outer suburbs via one of Perth's riverside cycle paths—or if you choose, you can take your bike to the outskirts on the suburban train. From there you will ride through part of the Swan Valley and ascend the Darling scarp through pleasant native woodland and pasture. There's some interesting colonial architecture in Toodyay and at York in particular, and some delightful farming country and gentle hills along the course of the Avon River. On your return to Perth you will visit Lake Leschenaultia and ride through

View of the city of Perth from Kings Park.

some impressive native forest between Mundaring Weir and
Kalamunda.

Start	Perth
Finish	Beckenham railway station (for Perth)
Distance	278 km (174 miles)
Duration	3.5–4 days
Terrain	The route is flat in Perth and along the Avon River from Toodyay to York, hilly going across the Darling ranges to Toodyay, and from Mundaring to Kalamunda. Undulating in the remainder.
Road Conditions	Generally good-quality roads, busy on outer suburban roads leaving and approaching Perth, otherwise quiet.
Accomm.	There areYHA hostels at Perth, York, and Mundaring Weir, and caravan and camping grounds, country hotels, B&Bs and farm stays.

Perth

Perth (pop. 1.2 million) is Western Australia's capital and
Australia's western gateway. It is one of the world's most
isolated cities, with Adelaide, its nearest sizeable neighbor,
2,120 km away. It was founded in 1829, when Captain James
Stirling formally took possession for the United Kingdom of
what was then known as the west of New Holland.

The first thing that strikes you about Perth is the wide,
blue Swan River and the fresh, clean look of the city. The
views of the city and surrounding areas from Kings Park are
stunning on a fine day—which is most of the time. The
climate is one of Perth's big pluses, with mild, sunny winters
and hot, dry summers. It is a great place to live and visit if
you like outdoor activities, particularly water sports. The
beaches are fantastic, with clean white sand, and the river is
well used by yachtsmen, water skiers, swimmers, divers, and
fishermen (though not all in the same place).

There are over 2,000 restaurants in the Perth metropolitan
area, and you can find virtually every kind of cuisine. The
main restaurant and nightlife area is Northbridge,
immediately north of the railway in the central city area. It
has a great atmosphere and is very cosmopolitan. There are

several backpacker and YHA hostels in this area, and the main YHA office is in William St. Northbridge.

There are some interesting old buildings left in Perth, but not many. A development-at-all-costs mentality in the 1970s and 1980s saw sandstone and wood give way to concrete and glass. Having said that, the tall, spare lines of the modern office block do give the city a striking profile against the river.

Much more interesting architecturally is the port city of Fremantle, which has had an active policy of conservation for many years. "Freo," as it is known, is a city of street cafes, old pubs, and a great market on weekends. In recent years it has become a mecca for artists and New Age people, though it proudly retains its multicultural working-class roots (to date a conservative politician has never been elected to represent Fremantle).

Apart from beaches, watersports, and coffee drinking in Fremantle, and living it up in Northbridge, there are plenty of other activities to enjoy during your stay. You can visit one of the local wineries, ride around the river on excellent cycleways, take a trip on a boat, or just do what you would do in any city—go shopping, see a movie, or relax in the park.

A word of warning—it's easy to stay longer than you intend in Perth, with its alluring climate and pleasant, laid-back atmosphere.

Day 1   *Perth to Toodyay*
(98 km/61 miles)

The first part of the ride out of Perth follows the suggested route in Ride 12 in the Bikewest publication "Around the Rivers Ride—Recreation Cycle Tour," except that I start the tour at the more centrally located Barrack St. jetty. However, if you wish to shorten your ride by approximately 24 km, you can take your bike down to Perth railway station and catch a train out to Guildford. From Guildford station, ride the short distance along James St. to Meadow St. and then rejoin the route description.

If you do wish to ride the whole way starting out via the Bikewest Ride 12, head east from the Barrack St. jetty along the cycleway by the river foreshore to the Causeway bridge. Ride under the bridge and follow the path past Trinity school. Continue along the path and pass under the rail bridge until you reach Summers St. Turn into Summers St. and take the first right into Joel Terrace. Follow Joel Terrace round to the

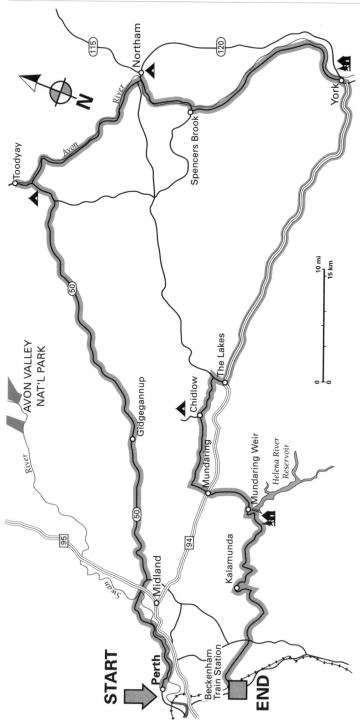

right, then turn right into Mitchell St. and left into Ellesmere Rd., passing St. Annes Hospital on the right.

Take the first right into Thirlmere Rd. and follow it as it bears left into Guildford Rd. Turn right onto Guildford Rd. (use the footpath) until you reach Third Ave. Turn right down Third Ave. and proceed past the stairs along Riverslea Ave. until you reach Fourth Ave. East. Turn right and descend steeply past Bardon Park until you reach the East St. T-junction. Continue straight ahead onto the dual-use path that runs through the foreshore rehabilitation area. At the end of the path turn left into Swan Bank Rd., then right into Peninsula Rd. Follow the path along Peninsula Rd. and then turn left at the Clarkson Rd. T-junction.

Follow the path round to the left along Hardey Rd. and continue onto the footpath that runs to the left of Tranby House. This path takes you along the riverbank past a block of units and turns left onto Swan View Terrace. Turn right and follow Swan View Terrace to its junction with Kelvin St. On the right you will see the dual-use path that will take you to Garrat Rd. bridge. You pass under the bridge then cross over the bridge. Turn left and follow the path as it takes you round the back of the Ascot racecourse and past the Ascot water playground. You then continue on the path over the boardwalk and through the rushes, until you come to Garvey Park.

From Garvey Park, you continue on the path on the foreshore, which ends 500 m later in Hilton Place. You turn left out of Hilton Place into Fauntleroy Ave., a quiet suburban street. Six hundred meters later, turn left into Hay St., where the cycle path resumes. The path takes you to a point where you ride parallel to but separate from the Great Eastern Highway—the busy main artery connecting Perth with Kalgoorlie and the eastern states.

At 24 km you come to a T-junction and traffic lights by the Guildford Hotel. Cross the main road (James St.) at the lights and turn right on the cycle path. Two hundred meters later, turn left at the traffic lights into Meadow St., cross the railway line, ride over the roundabout and into West Swan Rd. The road takes you past the Lilac Hill cricket ground on your right and occasional fields of grapevines. This is a part of the Swan Valley, Western Australia's oldest grape-growing and wine-producing area. A little farther along West Swan Rd., on the right you will see a service station and small shop. This is the last chance to buy food and drink without going out of your way, before you reach Gidgegannup 25 km further down the track.

At 28.3 km you turn right into Middle Swan Rd., which carries quite heavy traffic, and at 31.4 km you reach an intersection with the Great Northern Highway. Across the road to the right there is a cycle path. Take that path, then turn left into Bishops Rd. by a park, turn right into Lloyd St. a little farther along, and 200 m later turn left into the Toodyay road, which you basically follow until you reach Toodyay.

Soon you are riding through pleasant green pasture and native trees, and at 36.8 km from the Barrack St. jetty you start to climb for the first time. You wind your way up the Darling scarp for about 6 km through open marri woodland. The road then undulates, though you are still ascending over-all. The landscape here is a pleasant mix of green pasture and native woodland. At 51.5 km you come to the small settlement of Gidgegannup, where there is a service station and a roadhouse.

Just outside Gidgegannup, you enjoy a lovely long sweeping descent through farmland and stands of native trees. At 59 km there is a pleasant picnic spot at Noble Falls, where whitewater from a swift, flowing stream pours over rocks. From here the road rises and dips through pretty country, though there are also a couple of fairly demanding climbs. At 83.7 km you pass the Blinkbinney tea shop, after which there is a long and tiring climb followed by a 2 km descent, and then a fairly flat last 6 km into Toodyay.

Toodyay (pop. 800) was settled by white colonists in the early part of the 19th century. It is a quiet little town on the Avon River with some fine early buildings and historical sites to visit. There is a limited range of accommodation, which includes two older style hotels, the Avondown Inn (a restored convent offering B&B as well as backpacker accommodation), the Toodyay Caravan Park with camping ground, and a small number of farm stays. The pubs serve counter meals, and there are a couple of small restaurants and a very nice bakery. If you need cash, make sure you get to Toodyay during banking hours; I didn't notice any ATMs.

Day 2   Toodyay to York
         (65.5 km/41 miles)

Start by going back on the Perth road for 3 km, at which point you turn left on road No. 120, signed 27 km to Northam. This is a delightful road, winding through a shallow green valley with the Avon River in view on the left for much of the way. There is only occasional traffic, and the road is mainly flat with a good surface. There are no towns or settlements between Toodyay and Northam, but at 13.8 km there is an Alpaca stud farm that you can visit for a small fee. At 22.8 km you pass large concrete grain silos—Northam is a major rail center for transporting grain. You enter Northam at 27 km and cross the Avon River into town.

Northam, which is something of a regional center, is a town of over 7,000 people, quite large by Western Australian standards. There are plenty of places to buy refreshment or anything else for that matter. If you want to stay here there is a backpacker hostel called the Northam guesthouse at the corner of Grey and Wellington Streets.

To carry on to York, get yourself onto Wellington St. (parallel to the main shopping street), turn right and proceed out of town over the river. Just stay on this road, which will take you to York via Spencers Brook. This is a very quiet road that runs next to the railway line with only occasional traffic. Once again you will ride through a very pleasant agricultural valley with low green hills in the background. At 10 km out of Northam, you are signed left to York (27 km) just before Spencers Brook. This is a narrow but quiet country road, flat with a good fast surface. At just over 62.6 km from Toodyay, you pass York racecourse on your right, and at 64 km you enter the outskirts of the town. The town center is 1.5 km farther.

York, a lovingly preserved historic town, is Western Australia's first European inland settlement, dating back to 1831. It has many fine 19th- and early 20th-century buildings, a fantastic motor museum with some great classic cars, antique shops, galleries, a museum, and a couple of nice hotels. There is a very good YHA in Brook St., a caravan park, and numerous B&Bs and farm stays; the tourist bureau in Avon Terrace will give you a complete list. My friend and I were feeling affluent, so we stayed at the Imperial hotel ($50 for two.), an impeccably kept and friendly guest house that was formerly one of the old hotels.

Day 3   **York to Mundaring Weir**
       (80 km/50 miles)

Take the No. 194 Perth road out of York, and for the first 7 km
you will be mainly climbing through green farmland. Then
the road levels out and you enjoy a downward run for a
couple of km. This relief begins about 500 m past the sign for
York Golf Club. From here, the road is undulating for most of
the rest of the journey, with some long gradual climbs and
slow descents. The road is a good-quality two-lane country
highway with only occasional traffic.

From time to time the vista changes from green farmland
and low hills to native woodland. At 25 km from York you
pass through a fine stand of salmon gums, distinguishable by
the pinkish tinge and brown markings on their trunks. From
there to the Lakes you pass through a mix of farmland and
jarrah woodland.

The Lakes is a junction of the York road and the Great
Eastern Highway. There is a service station and roadhouse
where you can buy a sandwich or a cooked meal. From the
Lakes, turn right and proceed on the Great Eastern Highway
in the direction of Kalgoorlie. After 1.5 km turn left down
Doconing St., and 700 m later turn left again. You stay on this
quiet road to Chidlow, a small settlement with a tavern and a
general store set in pretty bushland. There are horses and
ponies, honey sellers and herb farms in this peaceful rural
setting on the far outer fringes of metropolitan Perth.

When you are in Chidlow it is well worthwhile making
the short detour to Lake Leschenaultia; it is only a few
minutes ride. It is signed to the right—either Rosedale Rd. or
Reservoir St. will take you there. Lake Leschenaultia is a large
freshwater lake, popular as a picnic and barbecue area. There
is also a camping ground.

From Lake Leschenaultia, return to Chidlow and turn
right when you reach the T-junction with the main street
(Thomas St.). You follow this road until you reach an
intersection at Helena Vale. Turn right into Lion St., then
100 m later left into Keane St. A couple of hundred meters
later you come to a four-way intersection. Cross the road into
McVicar Crescent, then veer right 100 m later into Keane St.
West. After a km or so, turn left into Sexton St. then right into
Riley Rd., signed 3 km to Stoneville. Proceed on this quiet
road to Stoneville, where you will come to a four-way
junction. Turn left into Stoneville Rd. Soon you will be

climbing for a couple of km before reaching the Great Eastern Highway at Mundaring. If you need any shops, turn right and you will find plenty 100 m or so down the road.

To reach Mundaring Weir, cross the Great Eastern Highway and follow one of the signed roads on the left. The weir is 7 km from the Mundaring townsite on a mainly downhill road through pretty state forest. The hostel is 50 m or so up a gravel track off the right of the Mundaring Weir road and is signed with a YHA sign.

The hostel is set in pleasant forest and has a well-equipped kitchen and a large lounge-dining area. Just across the Mundaring Weir road, up a steep hill, is the Mundaring Weir pub, which usually has a spit roast and a bush band on Sunday afternoons. Opposite the pub is a gallery that exhibits and sells arts and crafts. Also available from the hostel are Aboriginal cultural bush walking tours, courtesy of Djara Bush Tours.

Day 4 *Mundaring Weir to Perth via Kalamunda* *(34 km/21 miles)*

This short section completes the tour. It takes you through the forest, but then avoids much of the busy and uninteresting trek through the suburbs by taking you to a railway station, from where you reach the city center about a quarter of an hour later.

Turn right out of the YHA onto Mundaring Weir Rd., ride down a steep hill and then up an equally steep one to get out of the valley. Halfway up the climb there is a car park and lookout over the valley and the dam. From this point you climb for a couple of km through the forest, before the road flattens out and then follows an undulating course. The native forest is very attractive, and there are a number of picnic spots and barbecue areas. There are also some signs indicating patches of regrowth forest and the year that they were planted.

At about 10.3 km there is a nice descent of 2.7 km with views across a valley containing fruit orchards. At the bottom of the hill you curve round a sharp right-hand bend, then begin the 4 km climb into Kalamunda. This is best described as a moderate rather than tough climb; the gradient is not too steep, and the road surface is good. You wind and climb your way to a T-junction in Kalamunda opposite a shopping center, with the pub across the road to the right.

Kalamunda is a pleasant outer-Perth suburb set in the hills 24 km from the center of the city. You need to find Canning Rd. and turn left heading for Lesmurdie. After 2 km you come to a roundabout where you turn right and ride mainly downhill through Lesmurdie, another pleasant hills suburb, until you come to the Welshpool road, 6 km from the roundabout. Here you turn right and ride down the hill. It is a four-lane road and can get moderately busy. However, visibility is good and I would certainly not describe it as hazardous for cyclists. From this hill you get a great view of the coastal plain and the city in the distance.

At 29 km you come to traffic lights where the Roe Highway crosses the Welshpool road. Carry on through the lights until you come to William St., with Fremantle signed left. For much of the distance between Roe Highway and William St. there is a cycle path on the left. At William St. turn left and ride the last 3 km to Beckenham railway station. This is an awful road, very busy and full of big trucks. There is a cycle path on the left for the first few hundred meters. After that I would advise you to cross the road and ride along the footpath. It isn't the best of surfaces—old concrete flagstones—but it gets you out of the traffic. This last 3 km is simply a way of avoiding a much longer stretch of congested and uninteresting suburban road, by taking you to a railway station that will have you and your bike in the city center only a few minutes later.

When you reach Beckenham station, cross the line to the far side. Like most stations, Beckenham is unmanned, so you will need to buy a ticket for you and your bike from the machine. At the time of writing, both are counted as two zones adult rate, which will become clear when you read the instructions on the machine.

Bikes are permitted on trains between 9 A.M. and 3 P.M. but not at peak hours. The trains are swift and comfortable, and you will be in Perth in about 15 minutes.

Chapter 13.
Tasmania: Hobart to Devonport via East Coast

This tour takes you through some wonderful country on the eastern side of Tasmania. You will enjoy historic towns like Richmond and Swansea, experience some breathtaking coastal scener,y including the superlative Coles Bay and Freycinet Peninsula, and ride through lush and beautiful rain forests and agricultural pastures. You will also be able to explore Launceston, Tasmania's gracious second city and hub of the north.

Start	Hobart
Finish	Devonport
Distance	565 km (353 miles)

Salamanca Place in Tasmania's capital city, Hobart.

Duration	9–10 days (7 cycling days)
Terrain	The landscape is gentler than the rugged western side of the island (described in the tour that follows), but you will still do plenty of climbing, particularly in the northeast between St. Helens, Winnaleah, and Launceston. There are also flat stretches in the Freycinet Peninsula and along the east coast.
Road Conditions	Overall the roads are of excellent quality, quiet and very well signed, though the prevalence of a slightly coarse nonslip surface does make you work a little harder on some of the hills.
Accomm.	There are several YHA and backpacker hostels; budget hotels, caravan parks and camping grounds, B&Bs, and farm stays are also available.

Route Description

If you intend to combine this tour with the one that follows and ride right round the island, this is probably the best one to start on because it is a little less demanding than the western ride. Having said that, the order in which you proceed may be governed by your starting point in Tasmania—if you arrive in Devenport, there's no need to first travel across the island before starting your bicycle tour.

Day 1   Hobart to Triabunna
(90 km/56 miles)

This ride is a pleasant and relatively gentle introduction to cycle touring in Tasmania. You will pass through some pretty farmland, see some fine buildings in Richmond, experience a couple of tough climbs, wind through some forest country, and finally catch up with the coast toward the end of the ride.

You will quickly discover that road signage in Tasmania is second to none in Australia. All roads are numbered, and the state seems to have adopted the British system of large green signs, with road numbers in vivid yellow and the destination in clear white lettering.

Leaving Hobart, look for the A3 road to Sorell and the airport. I was staying at the youth hostel in King St. Bellerive on the eastern side of the Tasman bridge. In my case this meant a right turn into Petchey St. and onto Cambridge Road. This is a main road and at rush hour is quite busy. You soon join a four-lane freeway, which becomes less busy as you leave Hobart. It is quite good for cyclists, as it has an almost full-width emergency lane on the left, which allows you to separate from the traffic. There are some gentle ups and downs, and after 7 km on a long gradual descent you take the B31 to Richmond and Cambridge, clearly signed on the left.

Even though the A3 to this point is not terribly busy, it's always nice to get onto a country b road. The B31 to Richmond is fairly flat with a few undulations and views of the hills, which are fairly close on the left and further away to the right of the road. It's farming country here, a mixture of grazing and arable land and some rough pasture. The road surface is good, and you can work up a reasonable speed.

Richmond is a pretty, historic village with some fine stone buildings and Australia's oldest bridge (1823–1825) and oldest Catholic church. There are several antique and craft shops and lots of "olde worlde" B&Bs—at a price. It's a bit touristy, but very pretty and well worth the visit.

Leave Richmond on the B31 road toward Campania. The first 3 km are very flat, and you can reach a good speed. Seven km from Richmond, in pleasant farming country, you turn right on the C350 heading for the A3 East Coast road. A friendly bunch of roadworkers told me it was about 5 km to the A3—it was actually nearer to 7 km. These men were quite unusual in one respect, as nearly all country Tasmanians still think in miles.

You turn left on the A3 for Orford and after about 4 km encounter your first real climb, a steep winding ascent that the board on the summit tells you is called "Black Charlie's Entrance" and is 236 m above sea level. Enjoy the descent through forest and farmland, but prepare yourself for another stiff test 10 km ahead, aptly called "Bust Me Gall," a 336 m (1,000 ft) climb. If you intend to ride round the west of Tasmania, think of these two hills as a good early training run for bigger things to come.

After "Bust Me Gall," you will enjoy some steep descents through forested hills, some areas of which have been partially logged. A word of caution at this point—logging trucks use this road, and from here up to Orford and

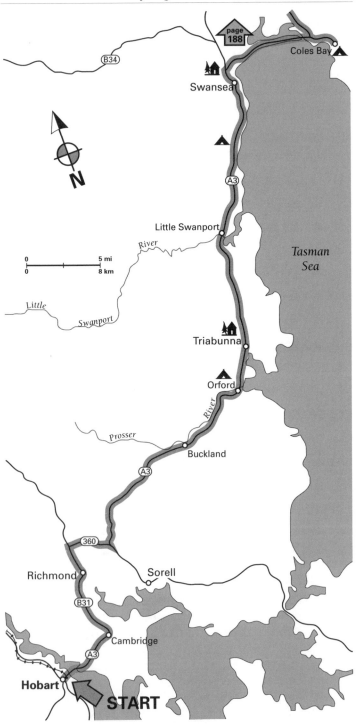

Triabunna you are likely to come across more of them. Generally it isn't a problem, but there are one or two narrow parts of the road where you need to take extra care.

Forty-one km from Richmond (64 km from Bellerive YHA) you come to the pleasant little village of Buckland, where you can grab a welcome drink or something to eat at the Shell roadhouse. On the day I made this ride it was cold, wet, and windy, so I was more than pleased to find a big log fire in the roadhouse cafe.

If you have the time to stop, Buckland has a very fine example of colonial church architecture in the church of St. John the Baptist. It was built in 1846 and has a beautiful east window said to have been originally designed for Battle Abbey in England on the site of the Battle of Hastings.

The first few km north of Buckland are through flat open country, with hills some way distant to the left and right of the road; but this is Tasmania, and soon you are climbing again through forested hills, then descending through pretty countryside. At about this point there is a road sign indicating 6 km of winding road. Be very careful here: the road narrows and there is an iron fence on the left, which gives you no space to make yourself scarce if a big logging truck comes thundering by. I didn't actually encounter any on this stretch, but I was listening hard for their ferocious rumble. If you do hear one behind you on this part of the road, my advice is to dismount and position yourself and your bike as close to the railing on the left as possible.

Notwithstanding the narrow road, the views here are great. Down below the road on the left, the ever-widening Prosser River flows beside a fine mature forest. After a winding descent, the road follows a flat course to the right of the river. The next section to Orford is very pretty, with the river, wooded hills, and winding road making almost picture-postcard scenery.

Orford, 80 km from the start of the journey, is a small coastal resort town that offers a variety of activities including fishing, walking, and sightseeing by charter boat. In former times when roads were few and far between, it was an important east coast seaport.

The A3 to Triabunna (signed to St. Marys) bears left over the bridge across the river. You pass the golf course on the left and enjoy your first ocean views on the right. A little further on, there are signs for the ferry to Maria Island, a former convict settlement and now a nature reserve, which I am told is great for walking.

Soon you enter Triabunna and turn right off the A3 to the town center. I stayed at the YHA, which is a short distance from the town center on Spencer Rd. The hostel is situated in a paddock behind the warden's house and has one dorm for men and one for women. There's a cozy lounge room and a nicely equipped kitchen. A bed costs $9 a night, and you can buy food items such as bread, eggs, fresh vegetables, fruit, and jam. There are also a couple of hotel-motels in Triabunna. I visited one of them, the Spring Bay motel, for an excellent counter tea and a couple of beers with the local fishermen.

Day 2   Triabunna to Coles Bay
(80 km/50 miles)

This day's ride is memorable for its beautiful views of the ocean, which you can hear, smell, and almost touch in places. You also pass through rich farming country with an ever-present vista of distant hills.

From Triabunna you rejoin the A3 coast road and turn right. The road has a good surface and carries very little traffic. After about 3.5 km there is a lake on the right—a wildlife reserve, teeming with ducks and other wild birds.

About 20 km from Triabunna you will see a sign on the left to Gum Leaves holiday and backpackers accommodation, 2 km down a dirt road. Ten km farther on, you catch your first glimpse of the ocean since leaving Triabunna, across green fields on the right. At Lisdillon a few hundred meters further on, "colonial accommodation" is advertised.

Five km from this point, you come to Mayfield Beach camping ground, a gem of a site right on the ocean, which rolls in with a big crashing surf. From here to Swansea the ride is quite delightful as the ride closely hugs the coast. There are little white sandy beaches and spectacular views of bays and rocky peaks.

Three km from Mayfield Beach you come across a real surprise. Perched on a low cliff right next to the surf is the Kabuki Japanese Tea House. Sheer curiosity makes a stop here irresistible. As you enter there are plenty of Japanese artifacts, paintings, and tinkling bells, but, at least when I was there, no Japanese people. A cheerful lady took my order for coffee and muffins while I sat next to the glass wall, watching the waves crash onto the beach a few meters away.

You continue on this lovely quiet coast road to Swansea, 59 km from Triabunna. Swansea is a small coastal resort town with plenty of useful shops including a chemist, a post office where you can draw on your Visa card, and a large general store. There are some fine old stone buildings too. Accommodation includes a backpacker's hostel at $12 per night, a YHA, and some more up-market B&Bs. There are also two cabin and caravan parks—the Swansea Kenmore cabin and tourist park and the Swansea caravan park and holiday village, both a good value, particularly if there are three or four of you.

While I was in Swansea I called the ferryman who operates across the narrow stretch of water from the end of Nine Mile Beach to the Freycinet Peninsula. His telephone number is (002) 570239. The drill is this: you call him to arrange a mutually agreeable time for him to pick you up. He will tell you to stand at the river's edge and wave your arms, after which he will bring his dinghy over and pick you up for $8. This is money well spent because it saves you a 60 km trip by road. Allow yourself about an hour from Swansea to the point where he picks you up.

To get to the pickup spot, you proceed out of Swansea on the A3 road for 4 km, where you will take the turnoff on the right signed to Nine Mile Beach and Dolphin Beach. Just under 2 km further on, there is a signed right turn to Nine Mile Beach. The road is predominantly flat and you will ride through low coastal scrub, with only the occasional glimpse of the nearby ocean. There are real estate agents' "For Sale" signs here and there, and it looks as if this particular spur of land is destined to become a site for holiday homes.

About 14 km from the turnoff from the A3, the road divides. Follow either road, as it is a loop. At the end you will find Bagot Rd., a short track to the river estuary. Take that, and then look across the water and attract the ferryman's attention. He told me that he has taken up to three bikes and riders across in his little aluminum boat, but two is a more comfortable limit. I was his only passenger on that crossing, which takes only about 5 minutes.

To get to Coles Bay Village, you follow the road from the river's edge for a hundred meters or so and turn right where it joins another road. The road curves and you turn left on the first road past some houses. At the next T-junction, turn right on a broad, well-surfaced road. Six km from the river's edge and the ferryman is Coles Bay Village. Almost 1 km before Coles Bay Village is the Coles Bay caravan park, which has a backpacker section at $14 per night.

At Coles Bay Village there is the Iluka holiday center, where you can get a cabin for $30 for two or $20 single. I stayed in one of these and was quite comfortable with a fridge, TV, hot plate, kettle, and cooking utensils. A few yards away is a row of shops that includes a supermarket that sells fish and chips, a tavern, and a pizza shop. There is also a small YHA where booking is essential. Because it is becoming a popular tourist destination, there has been a burgeoning of holiday accommodation here, from the Freycinet Lodge at $120–160 per person per night, to B&B and farm accommodation, none of which is in the budget range.

Coles Bay and other points on the Freycinet Peninsula are a must for a short stay if you are into bush walking or photography. Wine Glass Bay is perhaps the most famous piece of coastal scenery, but there are dozens of extraordinarily beautiful coastal and mountain views that make this part of Tasmania a real gem.

Day 3   Coles Bay to St. Helens
(115 km/72 miles)

This ride gives you a lovely mix of coastal scenery and farmland. There are no formidable hills, the road surface is good, and there is very little traffic.

The first 27 km of the journey take you up the Freycinet Peninsula to the point where you rejoin the main A3 coast road, 11 km south of Bicheno. Leaving Coles Bay I saw a sign warning of kangaroos for the next 25 km. I saw two live wallabies and sadly quite a few dead ones by the side of the road. On this stretch of road, you ride through forest and cleared farmland on the right and low coastal vegetation on the left, with views of the ocean inlet. On some parts of the inlet there were hundreds of black swans and other water birds. When I stopped to take a photo, the silence, punctuated by bird sounds, was pure magic. At 18 km from Coles Bay Village there is a sign right to the Friendly Beaches National Park, and at 27 km you rejoin the A3 road. There's more pretty farmland here, with fat merino sheep and grazing cattle. At the top of a rise just before the road curves down into Bicheno, you get a great view of the ocean.

Bicheno is one of Tasmania's most popular holiday resorts and is the center of an important fishing and abalone industry. The holiday brochures list boating, fishing, bushwalking, golf, horse riding, surfing, and sailing among its main attractions. There is a YHA and an excellent backpacker's section at Camp Seaview, $10 per night and close to the beach. There are also two caravan parks with on-site vans: Bicheno Campervan Park, at $25–30 for two; and Bicheno Cabins and Tourist Park, at $40 for two. There are numerous B&Bs from the high $40s per night, a couple of resort-style complexes and motels from around $35 per night.

The road from Bicheno stays close to the ocean most of the way to St. Helens, and the scenery varies from beautiful to delightful. Five km out of Bicheno there is a sign on the left to Douglas Apsley National Park, a 16,000-hectare park created to protect a large, relatively undisturbed area of dry eucalyptus forest. The park boasts spectacular waterfalls, gorges, and lookouts, and has a rich variety of fauna including pygmy possums and mountain dragons. A couple of km farther, there are tea rooms and a wild bird park. Another 2.5 km down the road, as you cross Dennison bridge you catch a glimpse of a lovely small white sandy beach.

Chain of Lagoons, which I recorded as just over 63 km from Coles Bay, is marked on the map, but there seemed to be nothing there except a stall selling crayfish on the right and a solitary farm. The turnoff to St. Marys (left on the A4) is here, and I stopped on a grassy patch near the turnoff to rest awhile and eat my lunch. I had seriously thought of going to St. Mary's but was so enjoying the coastal ride that I opted to press on to St. Helens. If you do go to St. Marys there's a steep climb called Elephant Pass, with a cafe at the top that is famous for its pancakes. The YHA at St. Marys is reputed to be very scenic, but to get there you have to travel 8 km from town uphill on a dirt road—unless the manager agrees to pick you up in his truck.

After my roadside lunch I pressed on to St. Helens. There are some gentle ups and downs but no tough climbs. To the left of the road there is forest and pasture, to the right, views of some lovely deserted beaches. About 14 km from the Chain of Lagoons is the Cray Drop In holiday village, which boasts accommodation at $40 per night for two, a restaurant, and a bar. At 86.3 km from Coles Bay there is a turnoff to Falmouth on the right. Falmouth is another small holiday town on this

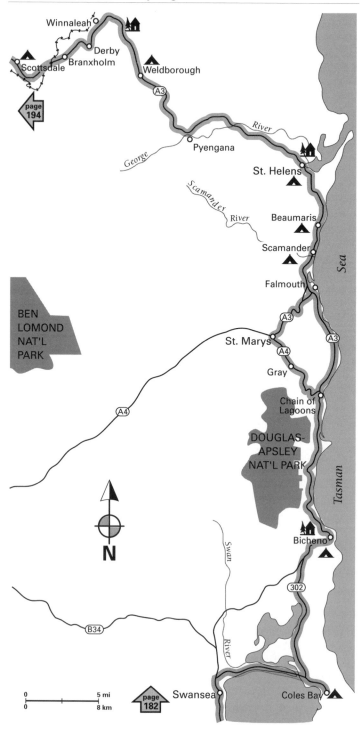

page
194

Winnaleah

Derby
Branxholm

Scottsdale

Weldborough

A3

River

George

Pyengana

St. Helens

Scamander

River

Beaumaris

Scamander

BEN
LOMOND
NAT'L
PARK

Falmouth

A3

St. Marys

A3

A4

Gray

A4

Chain of
Lagoons

DOUGLAS-
APSLEY
NAT'L PARK

Sea

N

Tasman

Bicheno

Swan

302

B34

River

0   5 mi
0   8 km

page
182

Swansea

Coles Bay

stretch of coast known as the Sunshine Coast. Don't follow the road to Falmouth, but instead curve left. The road narrows for the next 2–3 km, but it looks as if it is in the process of being widened. At the end of this narrow stretch you join the St. Marys-to-St. Helens road and turn right. There's a pleasant mixture of forest, farmland, and bush for 10 km until you come to Scamander, a small, spread-out holiday town with a population of 700.

Apart from swimming, fishing, and other water sports, the Scamander River is noted for its beautiful scenery along the estuary, and is a good place for bush walking. There are a lot of holiday units from about $28 per person per day, and a couple of motels. One of the motels that I passed was offering $39 per double, standby rate. Immediately, adjoining Scamander is Beaumaris, which also looks like a center for holiday units. The road runs parallel to the coastal reserve and white deserted beaches. Eventually it curves left through partly cleared forest, and you climb for 2–3 km before running down into St. Helens.

St. Helens is a busy little center that seems as though there are more than the official population of 1,005 people. I think I saw more traffic in 5 minutes in St. Helens than I had seen all day since leaving Coles Bay. Mind you, that is much more a reflection of the peaceful state of the roads than a suggestion that St. Helens is some kind of Los Angeles of eastern Tasmania. I stayed at the YHA, which is only a 5-minute walk from the center of town. The hostel is really just a largish suburban house with a big lounge room/kitchen area and a selection of fresh vegetables for sale. The town has a number of take-away cafes and a couple of pubs serving counter meals for around $10–15. I ate dinner at the local RSL club (a roast for $10).

Day 4   *St. Helens to Winnaleah*
(69 km/44 miles)

This ride takes you away from the coast and introduces you to some serious hill climbing. You will also get your first taste of some amazingly beautiful rain forest and end the day in green farming country.

You leave St. Helens on the A3 and enjoy a relatively flat first 3 km before coming to a fairly taxing climb for 1.3 km. The road then undulates through farmland, with some pleasant views of the surrounding hills. Farmland gives way to forest, and at the 7 km mark there's a well-advertised bric-a-brac and secondhand book shop all on its own.

Seven km later you come to a long, drawn-out hamlet called Goslen. There's an imposing roadside advertisement for the Tierview tea rooms serving "filter coffee" (obviously a rarity in this part of Tasmania) and "home-made German food." Unfortunately, I was unable to sample its delicacies because although it was 10 A.M., it was closed.

After the seemingly deserted Goslen, the road continues to wind through pasture, then forest. There's a long, steep climb through lovely tall timber, which descends into Pyengana, 28 km from St. Helens. On the outskirts of Pyengana you will see a sign to the famous "Pub in the Paddock" at Columba Falls, which is just as the description suggests. You can get B&B there for $25–30 per night. In Pyengana you will find a decent roadhouse where you can get meals and stock up on food, film, and any other common items. It's not a bad idea to have some high-energy food and drink here, as 3 km from the roadhouse you will begin a very demanding but beautiful 8 km climb through forest to the top of Weldborough Pass.

It is actually an exhilarating and enjoyable ride. It becomes tiring, but there are so many pluses—the road is quiet, the sound of the birds in the forest is delightful, and the scenery is magnificent. The road winds up the hills in a series of straights and curves, which is preferable in my view to those long straight climbs that seem to go on forever. As you climb, there are places where water splashes down rocks onto the road, and in one or two spots there are clearings that afford spectacular views of the countryside below. Eventually you reach the top of Weldborough Pass. You then reap your reward for the climb, a fantastic descent through rain forest complete with big tree ferns and lush undergrowth. From here, it's on to the little settlement of Weldborough, which consists of a few wooden cottages and a hundred-year-old pub.

I stopped for a welcome drink of squash, a steak sandwich, and a chat with some very personable locals. They told me that late in the last century Weldborough was a thriving mining center (tin and gold) and that there was a Chinese population of more than a thousand, who left when the ore ran out. There was a joss house that is now restored and is housed in the museum at Launceston. For some curious reason this lovely old low-beamed pub marketed itself as the "worst little pub in Tasmania" and offered a dubious menu with items such as "fart soup." I really liked the place and couldn't see why it would want to market itself so oddly. It is, by the way, residential at $18 single and $35 double, and there is also a camping ground at the back of the pub.

After leaving the pub, you head past a few cottages, and then at 47 km from St. Helens you hit Weld Hill, a steep, winding 6.5 km plunge through more wonderful rain forest. The road then flattens out and follows an undulating course to Moorina, which seems to be just a golf course on the left of the road. You then wind upwards through pretty agricultural land to a turnoff at 60.9 km, to Winnaleah signed 2 km to the right.

Winnaleah is a little agricultural village with a couple of general stores, a post office, a garage, a pub, and one or two other shops. The YHA is a further 6 km out of the village. You turn left past the post office as you face the church and follow the signs after that. The YHA is on a dairy farm on the right-hand side of the road. I was there on the Thursday before Good Friday, and the farmer's wife gave us homemade hot cross buns and chocolate animals. One of the other hostellers brewed a pot of Earl Grey tea.

Day 5   Winnaleah to Scottsdale
(48.2 km/30 miles)

This comparatively short ride includes some challenging hill climbs and exhilarating descents through attractive forest and farmland.

You start from the youth hostel by retracing your steps to Winnaleah and back to the A3 road, where you turn right. For the first few km you follow an undulating road through pretty farming country, then at about 12 km from the YHA you plunge down a steep winding 2 km descent through spectacular forested hills and gorges into the old town of Derby.

Derby is a classified historic town, which had its heyday as a tin mining center in the late 19th century. Some of the old mining buildings and equipment have been converted into a museum that documents a fascinating history of mining in northeastern Tasmania. Some of the town's shops sell crafts and antiques. I was struck by how old-fashioned Derby looked and by the beauty of its setting, surrounded by steep rocky gorges and trees. It was Good Friday, and apart from a couple of children playing on bikes in the street there was no one around—just a few slow columns of wood smoke from the chimneys of the little wooden cottages, and perfect silence. It was a lovely spot to grab a few minutes rest. If you want to stay here, there are a couple of old country-style hotels. There is also a general store if you need to buy any food.

After leaving Derby, the road follows the small Derby River for a while on a gently undulating road through forest and plantation country. At 21.5 km from Winnaleah YHA, you climb into Branxholm, then enjoy a longish descent through this small, drawn-out town. Six km further on there is a sign to Ledgerwood, 3 km on the left, advertising hostel and family accommodation. (Ledgerwood backpackers hostel is $12 per person per night.)

From the point where the road turns off to Ledgerwood, there is a long, gradual ascent followed by a steep climb and then a wonderful sweeping descent through a broad valley. At the 35 km mark there's another great 2 km descent, where you can easily reach speeds in excess of 50 km per hour. Farmland gives way to bush, and approximately 6–7 km outside Scottsdale you pass timber mills and other timber-processing places. Just before Scottsdale you will encounter a taxing climb, a descent, then another steep hill right to the town center and a road junction outside the Lords hotel.

This is where I stayed at $20 for a simple room and a self-serve continental breakfast. Scottsdale is perched at the top of a hill looking over farmland, with wooded hills in the middle distance. Lords Hotel is about the cheapest place to stay—and very satisfactory, with a little TV lounge and facilities for making tea and coffee. Other accommodation in Scottsdale includes a hotel-motel at about $35–40 per night, and a caravan park. There are several take-away cafes, a Chinese restaurant, and an RSL club. The town also has all the essential shops.

On the side of the Lords Hotel there is a sign that is a replica of a Thylacine (Tasmanian tiger). The northeastern part of Tasmania is where most sightings of this officially extinct animal have occurred. The official Tasmanian story (at least that put out in the tourist literature—not shared by the rest of Australia) is that the Thylacine is "extremely rare" or "on the endangered list." Like the canny Scots and the saga of the Loch Ness Monster, the people of Tasmania obviously recognize that the hope of spotting a Tasmanian tiger is no bad thing for tourism.

Day 6   *Scottsdale to Launceston via Lilydale* (71 km/44 miles)

This section takes you through more pretty farmland, with a few climbs to keep you on your toes. You pass close to some of the best-known Tasmanian vineyards and finish the day in Tasmania's elegant second city.

From the Lords Hotel you head down the A3 road to Launceston, through Scottsdale's main shopping street. After about 500 m there is a sign right to the Lavender Farm. Take that road. A few hundred meters farther on, you will see a sign to Lilydale, referring to the road that you are on. After leaving Scottsdale behind, a good two-lane road takes you through picturesque farming country, almost English in appearance and scale. At times the farmland gives way to forest and bush as the road winds and snakes on its way. There are a few hills and some pleasant descents. Just over 29 km from Scottsdale you will see a sign to Heemskirk, Pipers Brook on the right. This is one of Tasmania's most prestigious vineyards. In the Australian wine market Tasmanian wine is often hard to come by, but its better vineyards have the reputation of producing excellent cool-climate wines. At this same point on the road you begin a long, challenging climb, followed by a steep winding descent with great views into the village of Lebrina, 37 km from Scottsdale. There's a general store where you can stop for a drink if you need to, but the attractive bustling little center of Lilydale is only a few more km further on.

I stopped at a large supermarket/general store in the middle of Lilydale, housed in an old building. Outside the shop, a friendly man selling raffle tickets for a football club expressed a sentiment that I encountered all over Tasmania—why would anyone want to ride a bike round such a hilly place? Lilydale has a nice feel about it. There are a lot of craft shops and up-market B&Bs, and I suspect a sprinkling of middle-class alternative lifestylers. Fortified by food and coffee, I left the town behind to undertake the last leg of the journey to Launceston.

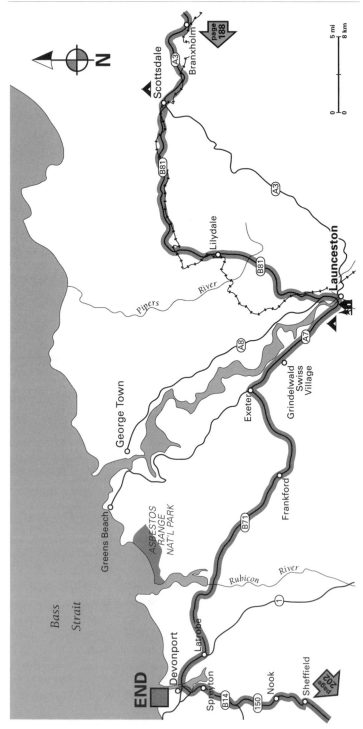

About 3 km out of Lilydale there's a long, demanding climb followed by some lesser climbs. A long descent takes you into Rocherlea, which from the increase in traffic and the bus stops you soon guess is an outer suburb of Launceston. The road becomes smoother and wider, and soon you join an urban freeway, though not a very busy one even on a Saturday morning. For much of the 5–6 km into central Launceston there is an emergency lane on the left, which makes an ideal cycling lane.

I had reserved a bed at the Launceston City Youth Hostel, which is an independent hostel not part of the YHA chain. It costs $11 per night and is housed in a vast former factory canteen building, one of the most unusual hostels that I have stayed in. The ground floor was full of weaving looms, timber planks, and hundreds of bikes, which can be hired along with an array of camping and wilderness equipment. To get there, find Wellington St., which is one of the main north-south streets in Launceston. You go roughly 2 km in a southerly direction, and on the way you will see a big factory building ahead on the right with the words "Coats Paton" on the side. You turn right down Throstle St. by a Trust Bank building. Throstle St. is cut by an urban freeway. You go over the footbridge, and in front of you on the building opposite the Coats Paton factory you will see the words "Launceston City Youth Hostel." There are also lots of old-fashioned pubs in Launceston, particularly in Wellington St. You can expect to pay around $30 per night for B&B.

Launceston is a city of more than 50,000 people, so you will have no trouble finding places to eat. There's a lot to see and do in this elegant old city: walking in the gorges, visiting the touristy but attractive Penny Royal Village and the museum, and taking in some fine city architecture.

Day 7   *Launceston to Devonport*
(92 km/57.5 miles)

Another mix of farmland, forest, and river views takes you to Tasmania's northern gateway.

Take the A7 road, the Tamar Highway, out of Launceston signed to Beaconsfield and Beauty Point. The first 6 km or so out of Launceston takes you through the suburbs on a four-lane dual carriageway. On the right is the river, with housing and vacant land on the left. At Legana, 13.3 km from the Launceston City Youth Hostel, there is a caravan park and a descent followed by the first real hill, a short steep climb of about 700 m. At this point there is a sign left to Grindlewald—a replica of a Swiss village—which is a residential development and holiday village. There are craft shops, chocolate shops, a Swiss-style bakery, a golf course, and canoeing. At this same point on the A7 there are signs right to vineyards and a wild bird park, which according to local sources is well worth a visit.

Seventeen km out of Launceston there is a hill approximately 1.8 km long, which is not too taxing, followed by a 3 km descent into Exeter. At the top of the hill there are great views of wide expanses of water and wooded hills, with Exeter in the distance. Exeter is a small town that serves a large rural district and important orcharding area. It has a supermarket, take-away food shops, and an excellent bakery situated on the right as you enter town. It sells among other things delicious berry pies, with berries that taste and look like a mixture of raspberries and blackberries. The only other place before Devonport where you can buy refreshment is a small service station at Frankford, 20 km from Exeter.

Continuing to Devonport, you take the B71 left off the A7. You travel on a quiet road through pretty farming country, where Hereford and Angus cattle occasionally lift their heads to watch you ride by. The outskirts of Frankford are signed about 16.5 km from Exeter, but the center—if that is what you can call the general store/service station and a couple of cottages—is 3 km further on, mostly uphill. The general store stocks a variety of food and drinks, and as I mentioned earlier is the last source of refreshment before Devonport. The countryside is a mix of farmland, forest, and plantation, and for the first 17–18 km out of Frankford you encounter a few climbs and descents, none of them too difficult. At 64 km out of Launceston, the C740, a gravel road, is signed right to the Asbestos Range National Park (12 km) and Bakers Beach (14 km).

Asbestos Range National Park is 4,281 hectares of coastal strip extending from Port Sorel to Greens Beach. It contains unspoiled beaches and coastline and is great for bird watching, bush walking, swimming, and horse riding. Wildlife includes the large Forester kangaroos, Bennetts wallaby, padmelon, and wombats. There are unpowered campsites at Bakers Beach and Griffiths Point at $6 per night for two people.

From here to Devonport the landscape is predominantly gentle farming country, a mixture of small pastures and rich arable land. As you approach Devonport the hills are rather gentler though the land is still undulating. Four km from Devonport you come to a crossroads. Devonport is signed left on a more major road, then right 500 m later when you join the A1—the main Launceston-to-Devonport road. You now descend into Devonport and encounter a busy road for the first time today. Cross the river Mersey and then leave the A1 on the left. Turn right and follow Formby Rd., which follows the Mersey into the middle of Devonport.

Devonport (pop. 25,000) is big by Tasmanian standards, the largest center on the northern coast. It is the home port for the Bass straits ferry, the *Spirit of Tasmania.* Needless to say, compared with most of the tiny centers that you have encountered in Tasmania, there is a wide choice of accommodation and food outlets. I stayed at the Tasman House backpacker's hostel in Steele St., which I can thoroughly recommend. For $8 I had my own (twin) room, which was cozy and spotlessly clean. The hostel used to be nurses' accommodation attached to a nearby hospital. It is very large but has a really friendly atmosphere. There's a big lounge/common room with a log fire, a TV area, and a big kitchen/dining area. From the center of town it's about 3 km

On Tasmania's east coast, you will ride along many deserted beaches like this one near Bicheno.

uphill on Steele St., just past the hospital. There is also a YHA hostel in Devonport and a number of older-style pubs that charge in the region of $30–40 for bed and breakfast. There are also at least three cabin and caravan parks: the Devonport Vacation Village in North Caroline St., the Mersey Bluff Caravan Park, and the Abel Tasman in Wright St.

Chapter 14.
Tasmania: Devonport
to Hobart via West Coast

This tour takes you through some of the wildest and most beautiful country in Australia. Part of the country you travel through is World Heritage–listed and national park. The old adage about "the more you put into something the more you get out of it" aptly describes this cycle tour. You will do plenty of climbing and some of it will really test you, but the

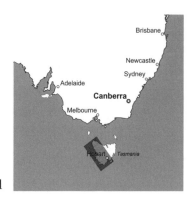

rewards in terms of breathtaking, rugged scenery are certainly worth it.

The tour takes in Cradle Mountain and the old mining towns of Roseberry, Zeehan, and the extraordinary Queenstown, surrounded by its bare rocky "moonscape." You will also visit Strahan, situated on the vast Macquarie

Leaving Tulach for Rosebery.

Harbour, the gateway to the Gordon River and adjacent wilderness area. In the latter stages of the tour you will enjoy fabulous scenery in your trek through the Franklin-Gordon Wild Rivers National Park up to the high country around Derwent Bridge. Finally you head southeast through forest and farmland down to Hamilton and Hobart.

Start	Devonport
Finish	Hobart
Distance	532 km (332 miles)
Duration	10 days (8 cycling days)
Terrain	The route is hilly/mountainous for much of the journey, but flat near the west coast and approaching Hobart.
Road Conditions	As in other parts of Tasmania, the roads are generally very quiet and of good quality. In some stages of this tour you will ride long distances where there are no shops or other outlets for refreshment. Where this is the case you will be clearly forewarned in the text so that you can set off well prepared.
Accom.	There are YHA hostels in Devonport, Strahan, and Hobart. In other places, you will find backpackers, country pubs, motels, B&Bs, holiday chalets, and campgrounds.

Day 1   *Devonport to Gowrie Park*
(44 km/27.7 miles)

This ride takes you almost halfway to Cradle Mountain through attractive farming country and some tall timbered forest. There are a few testing climbs and views of dark rocky mountains at the end of the ride.

Leaving Devonport, look for the B19 to Spreyton. From the Tasman House backpacker's this is simply a matter of going back down Steele St. toward the city center, then turning right at the roundabout into William St. For the first 8 km or so you are basically in the suburbs—Spreyton is an outer suburb. In Spreyton you turn right into the B14, signed 24 km to Sheffield.

At 9 km from Devonport you encounter the first real climb of the day, a testing 1.4 km. The landscape is the classic northern Tasmanian mix of attractive hilly pastures and forested slopes. At 13.5 km there is a sign to Nook, left on the C150. Local intelligence told me that going to Sheffield via Nook was quieter and had slightly more manageable hills, so I took the left turn onto the C150.

After leaving the Devonport suburbs the traffic had been quiet enough; from here to Sheffield on the C150 it was positively deserted. About 2 km after leaving the B14, there is a big twisting climb for 1.5 km through a stretch of beautiful tall forest. It's worth taking a break just to have a look around. The lack of traffic or other man-made sounds is good for the soul. After leaving the forest at the top of the hill, you ride down through farmland.

At 18.8 km there is a T-junction. Sheffield is signed 8 km right; Nook is signed left. I went left to Nook and wound through farmland on a flattish road. A little further along the road, you are signed straight on to Sheffield (6 km). About 500 m past this sign, round a 90° left-hand bend, the surface changes to a dirt road for about 2 km. Take care here because the dirt is almost the same color as the hard road surface and is difficult to spot. (I didn't, and nearly fell off down a slight hill.)

The road winds right, and after climbing a hill and then descending through some trees, you hit the hard surface again. A little further on, after climbing a slight hill there is a sign to farm accommodation on the left. From here you coast down to Sheffield, though you actually see it a couple of km before you get there. It sits in a valley, with dramatic rocky peaks on the horizon.

Sheffield is a lively, bustling little town that is obviously attuned to the tourist trade. It is set in very attractive countryside close to pleasant farmland and rocky mountains with waterfalls and gorges, which makes it excellent for bushwalking. It is also close to the Lake Barrington international rowing course. The surrounding lakes and rivers make it a good base for trout fishing and water sports. A feature of the town is the 32 murals depicting different aspects of the town's history. Some of them can be seen in the center of the town.

If you contemplate staying in Sheffield to explore its environs, there is plenty of B&B accommodation, though not much of it in the budget range. There is backpacker accommodation for $15 per night at the Sheffield Country Motel; on-site vans at the Sheffield Caravan Park cost $25 per

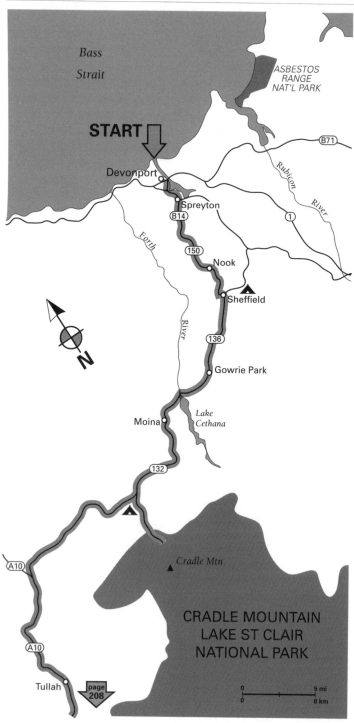

Bass Strait

ASBESTOS
RANGE
NAT'L PARK

B71

START

Devonport

Rubicon

Spreyton

River

B14

1

Forth

150

Nook

Sheffield

River

N

136

Gowrie Park

Lake
Cethana

Moina

132

A10

Cradle Mtn

A10

CRADLE MOUNTAIN
LAKE ST CLAIR
NATIONAL PARK

Tullah

page
208

0   5 mi
0   8 km

night for two, with fees for the hire of linen and pillows. There are plenty of shops selling food and other provisions. You would be well advised to buy food for your evening meal as there are no shops of any kind at Gowrie Park. However, there is a restaurant there, with main courses in the $14–20 range.

To proceed to Gowrie Park, you first follow the sign to Railton (the B14). A few hundred meters further on, Gowrie Park and Cradle Mountain are signed right on the C136, Gowrie Park 14 km. Just over 3 km out of Sheffield on this quiet road, there is a sign to holiday accommodation, though no details are given. Half a km later, Paradise is signed 3 km on the left.

Six km out of Sheffield you pass through a hamlet called Claude Road, which appears to have a tiny fire station and a memorial hall and nothing much else. A little further on there is a sign on the left to the Silver Ridge Retreat, boasting self-contained serviced cottages with an indoor heated pool close to bush walks. Just over 5 km later you arrive at Gowrie Park, which appears to be no more than a couple of logging operations and an office of the Hydro Electric Commission.

Notwithstanding the fact that it is not much more than a dot on the map, the setting of Gowrie Park is striking and spectacular with its background of rocky peaks, forest, and bushland.

The backpacker hostel used to be the single men's quarters attached to the Hydro Electric Power Commission. It is a vast and slightly run-down affair, but a great value at $8 per night for your own lockable cabin. There's a big kitchen and a large mess room with a fireplace and a supply of logs. If nobody seems to be about when you arrive, veer left down Wellington St. to the Weindorfer's restaurant. The lady there will take your money and give you your key.

Day 2   *Gowrie Park to Cradle Mountain*
(40 km/25 miles)

Before I set out on this section, I confess to being somewhat apprehensive. The image and reputation of Cradle Mountain conjures up impossibly tough climbs and wild weather—a time to sort out the men from the boys, so to speak. The reality is a challenging and exhilarating day's riding through some wonderful country, with outstanding views of rugged forest and striking rocky peaks and ranges.

From the backpacker's at Gowrie Park, turn left toward Cradle Mountain. The first 4–5 km takes you through forest with high peaks on the left. This first section has some gentle climbs, then a slightly more difficult one. At 5 km out there is a sign right to Cradle Vista accommodation 3 km and farm accommodation 11 km. Just after this point, you embark on a thrilling 3 km winding descent through the forest down to a bridge across a wide river. Then, of course, you have to pay the price for this all-too-fleeting pleasure—7 km of twisting, tough if not tortuous climbing.

This was probably the toughest climb that I came across in Tasmania, but it is also one of the most scenic, with great views behind you across rocky ridges and gorges. Try to pace yourself on this climb. Unless you are super fit you will need to stop for a break a few times. While you are having a rest, take time to enjoy the view; it makes all the hard work worthwhile. I didn't know exactly how long the hill was, and I was just beginning to wonder if I would ever make it to the top when I saw a wonderful roadside sign, "Tea Room 400 m." The ordeal was over. There are actually two tea rooms at the top of the hill.

This place is called Moina and is the site of a former mine and settlement now long gone. The C136 on which you have been traveling joins the C132. Turn left to Cradle Mountain; Wilmot is to the right. You continue to climb for another 3.7 km, but it feels like a picnic after the monster that took you up to Moina. Two km out from the tea rooms there is a sign to Lemonthyme Lodge, described as wilderness accommodation. The country from here is more open, a mixture of logged forest and pasture, which has less of a lush appearance as you climb higher. Disappointingly, as you come within 20 km of Cradle Mountain a lot of the country has been logged. In parts you ride through a landscape of stumps and dead trees, which can look particularly forlorn in the slanting rain.

The turnoff left for Cradle Mountain is 21.3 km from the Moina tea rooms and is well signed. Immediately past the turnoff, a large information board tells you exactly how far things are—e.g., camping ground 3 km, Cradle Mountain Lodge 6 km. As the board indicates, 3 km further on, the camping ground is signed on the right. At this point there aren't any views of Cradle Mountain itself. There are better vistas near the lodge, but the actual mountain is 5 km beyond the lodge.

Probably as a consequence of the law of supply and demand, the camping ground and bunkhouse section are relatively expensive here. I paid $20 for a bed in a cabin shared by three others, and $10 for blankets. Although the cabins are small, they are clean, with two double bunks and an electric heater. There is an excellent modern shower block, a cooking shelter with barbecue tops and hotplates, and a small, warm common room at the end of one of the bunkhouse buildings. The whole thing is set in very pleasant bushland. A word of warning—there were no pots and pans, plates, or cutlery for communal use. If you plan to cook dinner or even have a drink you will need your own utensils.

I walked down to the lodge for a drink and had dinner there in the evening. Cradle Mountain lodge caters for the mid- to up-market tourist market—the barman told me that visitors from Sydney accounted for 80% of their customers. Accommodation both in the self-contained cabins and the lodge itself is relatively expensive—$95 to $140. You can get a meal in the bar/bistro for about $11–15 for a main course. Also at the lodge there's a shop where you can buy provisions, but there is a bit of a mark-up on most items. There is bunkhouse accommodation at Waldheim 10 km further on from the lodge. There are eight cabins accommodating 4–8 people. Cutlery and crockery are supplied, but pillows and linen are not. The daily charge is $19 per person.

Cradle Mountain is part of a world-famous wilderness area and is a mecca for walkers, rock climbers, and photographers, but you don't have to be too much of a pro. Around the lodge there are several signed walks of varying length for people who don't have time for 3-day treks. Even if you are not planning to stay long, it is well worth taking the time to walk through this lovely wilderness country.

Day 3   *Cradle Mountain to Rosebery*
(69 km/43 miles)

Before setting out on this stage of the tour, you would be well advised to make sure you have some provisions at least for the first part of the ride, as there is no opportunity to buy anything before reaching Tullah 54 km from Cradle.

I set off in an icy driving rain, but as is so often the case in Tasmania, the rain that day was a very on and off affair and didn't spoil another magnificent day's ride through rugged mountainous country, bushland, and lush forest on the outskirts of Rosebery.

Initially you retrace your steps to where the Cradle Mountain turnoff meets the C132. The C132 road is quite new—around five years old. It is an excellent road, but once again it has that coarse nonslip surface that makes it a bit harder for us cyclists.

After 5 km of greeny brown heathland with scattered trees, you enjoy a 2 km descent, cross a cattle grid, and climb a hill, gently at first, then very steeply for 700 m. This is Black Bluff, the steepest but not the longest climb of the day. You are rewarded by a 2 km descent through bleak heathland, with great views of big rocky peaks in the distance. This is quite wild country, and there are no houses or signs of human activity as far as the eye can see.

At 30 km out from Cradle, after leaving the heathland and traveling through bush, young forest, and plantations, you arrive at a T-junction where you join the A10 road. You turn left signed to Queenstown and Tullah (24 km). On the way to Tullah there are a few minor climbs and some great descents. At just over 32 km you wind down a 6 km descent through bush and low forest. There are other good descents at 45 km and 47 km.

As you approach Tullah the views become more spectacular, with rocky peaks in the background. At 53.6 km you reach Tullah. It is a small settlement in mountain country with a pub that sells hot food. When I stopped for a squash and a pastry, I couldn't help noticing the stickers behind the bar, many of which were not at all kind to Greens. One proclaimed "Fertilize the Wilderness: Doze in a Greenie!" But like all Tasmanian country pubs that I'd been in, it had a big log fire, which was very welcome on a cold, wet day.

After leaving the pub, you ride by a couple of lakes or dams, which look quite striking set against a backdrop of jagged peaks half covered in mist. You will see "lakeside accommodation" signposted 3 km to the right just after leaving the pub, as well as a motel at $30 per night standby rate. The road out of Tullah is flat for the first couple of km, and you pass a sign indicating straight on to Rosebery (left to Queenstown).

At 60 km, by a road sign signifying an 8 km winding road, you begin a 3.8 km slow climb through steep forested country. There are lush tree ferns growing at the side of the road and little streams of water splashing down the rocks. In fact, as you slowly wind your way up you hear the constant sound of splashing water. After the climb, you enjoy a fabulous finale to the day's ride, plunging over 4 km through this wonderful mountainous tree-covered country into Rosebery, which lies at the bottom of a valley encircled by dark, rocky peaks.

Rosebery owes its economic life to mining—zinc primarily. It was founded on the discovery of gold in 1893 and named after Lord Rosebery, the British prime minister. It has a long, downward-sloping main street with two pubs, a bank, and a variety of shops. It could be any one of many Australian country towns except for its absolutely magnificent wild mountainous setting.

I stayed at the Rosebery hotel, which is advertised in a backpacker accommodation leaflet entitled "Budget Beds Tasmania." A clean, simple hotel room is $15 ($22 with cooked breakfast). The pub serves counter meals, and there are a number of small cafe/take-aways in the main street; there is also an RSL club. For alternative budget accommodation you could try the caravan park, which has a cabin section.

If you stay in Rosebery, it's a good center for bush walking and fishing. There is also a golf course and tours of the local mine three times a day for $8 (the bus leaves opposite a cafe cum craft shop at the top of the street).

Day 4   *Rosebery to Strahan via Zeehan*
(74 km/46 miles)

Today your ride begins with more spectacular mountain scenery, which changes to bare hills and button grass as you approach Zeehan, an old mining town. From Zeehan it's a flattish ride through more button grass hills and then coastal dunes, before arriving at the lovely coastal town of Strahan, the gateway to the Gordon River.

From the Rosebery hotel you head down the hill and curve right through South Rosebery. You then climb slightly, with steep forest on either side. There's a little railway on the right, no doubt connected with one of the mines. At 4 km you pass the soft green expanses of the Rosebery golf club— quite a contrast to the dark forest and rocky mountain peaks. You climb again, and at 9 km you pass a sign telling you that you are close to one of the world's biggest tin mines (Renisons). The sign urges you to enjoy the scenery over the next 7 km, which is their lease. Just after the 10 km mark you encounter

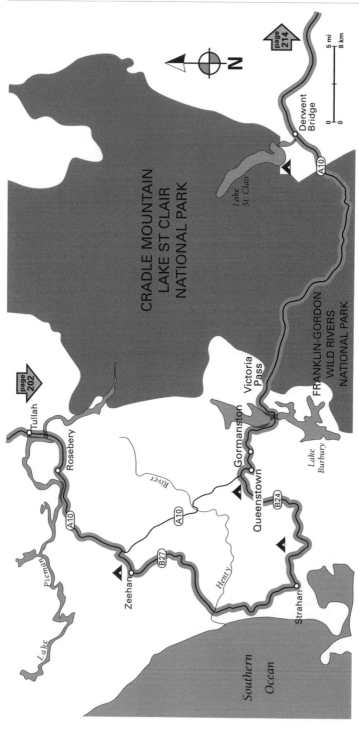

a steep 1.5 km climb, which takes you to the tin mine at the top of the hill. Just round the corner is a sign, "Battery Mill Historic Walk 500 m on Right."

The road is quite spectacular, winding its way through a steeply wooded valley, which at certain points you can see far into the distance like a big, green trench. This part of the ride is characteristic of much of Tasmania, rising and falling, with climbs rewarded by some speedy descents.

At 23.4 km you arrive at a T-junction, with Zeehan signed clearly right, 7 km on the B27. The landscape changes, and trees are replaced by hills with a thin cover of green vegetation and brownish button grass. I was now conscious of descending despite the repeated ups and downs. At 27.8 km you hit the outskirts of Zeehan and the sign left to Strahan. I was keen to take a look at Zeehan, so I pressed on to the town center a further 2 km away. As you proceed toward the center you pass the Heemskirk Motor Lodge on the left and the Zeehan Motor Hotel and backpacker lodge further on on the right, as the road curves right.

Zeehan is an interesting old town with a few shops, a bank, and a huge old post office building. Well worth a visit is the Zeehan Mining Museum, housed in what was until the early 1960s the Zeehan School of Mines. I found the many old black-and-white photographs of mining, rail, and maritime activities fascinating.

I retraced my steps to the outskirts of town and took the well-signed B27 road to Strahan (43 km). The first 4 km is very flat, if not downhill, judging by the speed you can reach. The landscape is characterized by a mix of button grass and green jagged hills. At about 10 km from Zeehan, there is a climb followed by a descent and then more very flat road with some long straight stretches (a novelty for Tasmania). There is more button grass and sparse trees—very different from the spectacular wooded valleys at the beginning of the day's ride.

After arriving at the top of a rise 22 km out of Zeehan, you get a nice view of the ocean and pass a sign indicating a turnoff to Ocean Beach. You descend the hill and encounter more flat stretches. After crossing the Henty River, you ride through pine plantations and low coastal scrub. You enter Strahan just over 74 km from Rosebery. Soon after you come into Strahan, the YHA is signed clearly on the left at the beginning of Harvey St.

The YHA has been extended and modernized. There are new timber dorms and a large and comfortable kitchen/lounge area, which is very well equipped with two fridges, a microwave, two 4-burner gas stoves, a cool drinks machine, and a wood stove. There is also a laundry with a coin-operated machine, modern shower blocks, and a range of food and toiletries for sale at the reception.

The Strahan waterfront and shops are a 10-minute walk up Harvey St. from the YHA. Situated on the very picturesque waterfront is an excellent general store/supermarket, a bakery, and pizza shop with an array of delicious freshly baked items, a butcher, a photography and gift shop, and Hamers Hotel, which serves good counter meals in its bistro. There are also a variety of activities on offer including cruises on the Gordon River, sea-plane trips, 4WD expeditions, horse riding, and fishing. If you intend to take a trip on the Gordon River, it is advisable to book at least a couple of days in advance as they are usually fully booked. There are two companies that run cruises down this famous wilderness river.

Apart from the YHA there is a fair quantity of holiday accommodation in Strahan, from hotel/motel to B&B and holiday cottages for rent. Strahan is becoming a very popular tourist destination, so if you want to do B&B or rent a cottage, make sure you check the latest prices—some of them may be quite high.

There is a lot worth checking out in Strahan. It is a delightful little town with a grand past, and of course it is the gateway to some of Tasmania's and Australia's most breathtaking wilderness country. You'll probably want to stop over here for a day or two.

Day 5   Strahan to Queenstown
(42 km/26 miles)

This 42 km stretch through Tasmania's "wild west" is quite a tough little ride, with plenty of climbing to keep your blood pumping. Once again, though, you are rewarded with some wonderful mountain scenery and a quiet road.

From the YHA, you ride up Harvey St. and turn left at the top on the B24 signed to Queenstown. You climb for about 6 km, winding through forest. After this the road undulates, but overall you are still climbing. At about the 13 km mark you briefly cycle through open grassland where you have views of big jagged peaks ahead and to the right. However, the road is soon enveloped again in dense growth, mostly small trees and bush. For a couple of km here, the road is quite rough at the edges, and in parts, it slopes steeply to the left; however, it is quiet, with very little traffic.

At about 22 km from Strahan there is a rather steep climb of about 800 m. You get glimpses of distant mountain scenery, and at 24 km there is a scenic lookout on a bend, with spectacular views high above a valley to mountains beyond. For the next km or so you enjoy fine views on the left before trees enclose the road again.

The route twists and turns, and at about the 28 km mark I came across bare, burned hills and scrub to the right as if a fire had recently been through there. There are views of huge bare rocky hills, but as yet no sight of Queenstown.

At just over 37 km from Strahan, the B24 joins the A10 Burnie-Queenstown road. You turn right as signed and descend the last few km into Queenstown, which sits at the bottom of a valley surrounded by bare (environmentally degraded) rocky hills. Soon after you enter Queenstown, you encounter the Mountain View Motel and backpackers on your right. This is where I stayed. You get a lockable twin cabin for $9 per night. There's a large, basic kitchen and a shower block that is better than it looks.

Other places to stay in Queenstown include the lovely old Empire hotel, which has rooms at budget prices; the historic Hunters Hotel; the Mount Lyell Motor Hotel; and the Queenstown Cabin and Tourist Park, which has cheap bunkhouse accommodation or a space on the floor for a few dollars. There are plenty of useful shops, a number of cafes and take-aways, and counter meals at the pubs.

Queenstown is a classified historical town and the main center of the west coast. Condemned by some as an example of extreme environmental degradation due to unfettered mining activity, the bare rocky hills that surround the town nevertheless lend it a certain bizarre charm—at least that was my view as a passing visitor. With its fascinating history as an isolated mining center—it was not linked by road to Hobart and the east coast until the late 1930s—Queenstown has the air of real character and independence.

Day 6   **Queenstown to Derwent Bridge**
(87 km/53 miles)

This is a day of lakes, mountains, and wild beautiful scenery which ends in the high country at Derwent Bridge. It also seems like a very long ride, because after Gormaston just outside Queenstown you don't see a single building of any kind until you reach Derwent Bridge. There are no towns, roadhouses, shops, or houses visible from the road. So be warned—take some food with you and make sure you have plenty of water.

After turning right out of the Mountain View Holiday Lodge, take the first left, signed for Hobart, climbing very slowly at first, then more steeply as you approach the mountain. The way out of Queenstown up the side of the mountain looks awesome. On the day I did it, it looked positively dramatic, with the tallest peak over on the right, Mt. Owen, covered in snow. The climb is actually not too bad: it is steep in parts but looks worse from the bottom than it is—and there are opportunities at some of the hairpin corners to enjoy spectacular views while you stop and rest for a moment. The sound of distant trucks or buses above or below straining to climb the hill adds to the dramatic effect, but there are some parts of this climb where the road is quite narrow, so take care if you do see or hear a big truck approaching. While safely resting off the road halfway up, I observed a big semi cover every inch of both sides of the road in order to get itself round a corner.

The climb to the top of the mountain is 5 km before you descend 2.5 km through Gormaston, a small mining settlement. Just through Gormaston, on the left, there is a tea room cum woodcraft shop. The coffee isn't the greatest in the world, but it is the last source of refreshment for 80 km.

After leaving the tea shop, you enjoy about 4 km of flat road as you ride along the bottom of a valley. Then on your left you come to Lake Burbury, a large, spectacular lake edged by mountains. You continue on a flat road along the side of the lake, then cross the lake on a long, low bridge. Once across, you encounter a few small climbs and descents through wonderful scenery, with views of mountains and the lake. Twenty-five km out of Queenstown there is a sign telling you that for the next 50 km you are in the Franklin-Gordon Wild Rivers National Park. Three km further on there is a car park for people wanting to visit Nelsons Falls via a signed walk. As you enter the national park, the bare, rocky hills and button grass give way to trees and lusher vegetation. At about 28 km you begin a 3.5 km ascent to the top of Victoria Pass, which begins to test you as you near the top.

After descending from Victoria Pass, you ride along an undulating road through forest country. You are joined by the Collingwood River on your left for a while, and later the Franklin on your right. At 52 km, close to the top of a tough climb, there is a sign to the right—"Doaghty's Hill Wilderness Lookout 40 minute return walk." There are a number of other walks signed along this part of the ride.

At 76 km, after climbing for quite some time, you see a roadside sign proclaiming "Mt. Arrowsmith." There is a further 5 km climb, which although not in the super-tough category, is quite taxing coming as it does toward the end of the day's ride. At the top of Mt. Arrowsmith the land is like heathland, with tufts of brown and green grass. In the last few km to Derwent Bridge, the heathland gives way to more trees, and the landscape looks generally greener.

Derwent Bridge isn't much more than a dot on the map. As far as I could see, it consisted of the Derwent Bridge Hotel, a service station, a couple of holiday cottages, and very little else. I stayed at the Derwent Bridge Hotel, which has a large number of backpacker cabins at $15 for a lockable cabin with a small heater. The hotel has a huge log fire and comfortable chairs and sofas. The inside of the hotel is open plan, with a big dining area and lounge bar partially separated from the public bar by a wall and the fireplace. It was warm and cozy on that cold day and served an excellent meal at bistro prices: $11–18 for a main course, soups $4.50. A serve-yourself breakfast was also available for $8—juice, cereal, toast, and coffee. There is other backpacker accommodation in the Derwent Bridge area at the Lakeside Holiday Cabins at Cynthia Bay from $15 per person. There is also a camping ground at the same location.

Day 7   Derwent Bridge to Hamilton
(104 km/65 miles)

This day's ride takes you down from the high country to the lush hilly farmland of the Hamilton district—but it's certainly not downhill all the way. You will tackle a few tough climbs and see more great scenery on a generally peaceful road.

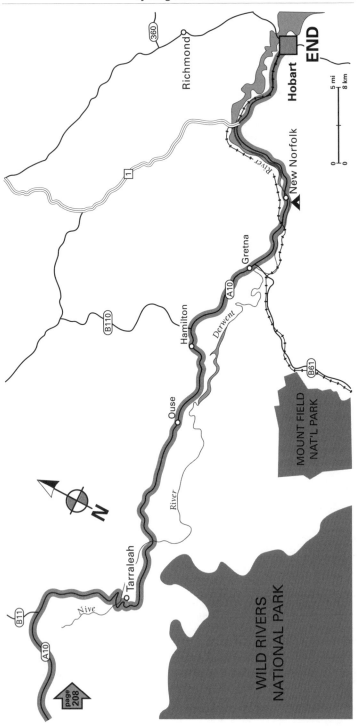

I left the Derwent Bridge Hotel and turned right on the A10 to Tarraleah and Hobart. Almost immediately there is a sign on the left to Lake St. Clair (5 km), for those who might wish to visit this famous lake. Continuing on the A10, the first 20 km is either flat or slightly downhill, which allows you to work up a good speed as you cycle through brownish heathland and partially logged forest. You encounter your first serious climb at 24 km after a swift descent. At just over 26 km you will notice a sign on the left—the B11 to Bronte Park Highland Village, where there is accommodation and meals. The backpacker hostel there charges $12 per night, or you can get a cottage for $16 per person per night. At 28 km you see Brady Lake on your left, which looks spectacular against a hilly backdrop. Five km further along the lake, there is a whitewater canoe course and boat ramp.

At 42 km from Derwent Bridge, there's a swift and dramatic 4.2 km descent through tall trees to an electricity generating station at the bottom of the valley. You then pay for this 5 minutes of speedy pleasure by grinding your way up the other side of the valley for 3 km. A little further on, you come to a road on the left signed to Tarraleah Village. If you want to buy food and drink, follow the road to the village, which is about 500 m from the turnoff.

Tarraleah is a residential village for the workers at the Tarraleah-Tungatinah power station. Follow the road as it curves to the right. Halfway up the hill on the right, there is a road on the right-hand side where there is a supermarket and cafe that sells hot food.

To rejoin the A10 to Hamilton, carry on up the hill through the village. The road curves right, and you rejoin the A10 just past the Ampol service station and roadhouse. You continue to climb for a couple of km through forests and plantations, then plunge 4.5 km to a bridge over the Nive River. There are signs right here to Wayatinah Village camping ground and picnic area. The camping ground has 50 sites (24 of which are powered) sewered toilets, washing machine, heated pool, camp kitchen, barbeque, and tennis courts. If you want to make a stopover, Wayatinah offers bush walking, squash, golf, and many scenic lagoons and lookouts.

From the bridge over the Nive River, you climb a testing hill through forest, then at the 76 km mark there's a 5 km descent. The landscape has changed to farmland with fields of sheep and cattle, interspersed with occasional patches of forest. There are no more significant climbs from this point; in fact, the road is generally running downhill. You arrive at the town of Ouse at 89 km. You could stay here—there's accommodation at the pub, and you'll see quite a few signs on the road to cottage or farm stays.

I decided to press on the few more km to Hamilton. At 97 km the road to Ellendale is signed on the right, together with a number of places to stay. This is an alternative route to Hobart. I continued on the A10 through the easygoing farmland and entered Hamilton at 104 km from Derwent Bridge.

Soon after you come in to Hamilton there is a sign left to the Hamilton Inn. This is where I chose to stay, though there are also quite a few B&B cottages in Hamilton. The Hamilton Inn is a fine 100-year-old pub built of stone, where bed and breakfast costs $30. The room was very cozy with a wall heater and an electric blanket, which I was glad of on a chilly evening. There's a cozy bar with a roaring log fire and a good choice of main courses for dinner. I had a great meal by the fire in the dining room, and contemplated that this would be my last night before the end of the tour.

Day 9   Hamilton to Hobart
(71.5 km/45 miles)

This last day's ride takes you down through farmland to the Derwent River, the historical center of New Norfolk—famous for its spring flowers—and finally on to Hobart.

Hamilton sits in a shallow valley, so for the first 4 km you climb out of it through pleasant grazing land. At around the 7 km mark, a double bonus awaits you—a finer, faster road surface and the beginning of a 13 km descent to Gretna through gentle farming country. Gretna is a small town or village with a general store, service station, and pub—the Gretna Green.

You climb out of Gretna (the last part of the climb is very steep) to the neighboring village of Rosegarland, which appears to be just a collection of cottages and a pub. As I stopped for a breather, a laden log truck rumbled past. I had encountered quite a few of these monsters since leaving Hamilton, but experienced no difficulty or anxiety on this otherwise quiet, good-quality road.

After Rosegarland you meander down to the broad, swift-flowing Derwent River. There's a picturesque little wooden church-like building on the river's edge and a line of poplar trees along the side of the road, which looked very pretty in their autumn gold. The road follows the river to Hayes, which hosts Tasmania's only prison farm.

About 5 km further on, you enter New Norfolk, an historic regional center of over 6,000 people. There are plenty of shops as well as a couple of historical "firsts." St. Mathew's church is reputed to be the oldest Anglican church in Tasmania, while the Bush Inn hotel claims to be the oldest continuously licensed hotel in Australia.

Leaving New Norfolk for Hobart, the road becomes busy. It is flat, following the river to the outer suburbs of Hobart. This last stretch is not great bike riding, especially once you hit the outer suburbs. It is simply the way to the end of the ride. Nineteen km from Hobart you join the A1 Launceston-to-Hobart highway, which becomes a four-lane freeway. The traffic is quite heavy, but for much of the remainder of the journey you will find a space to the left of the traffic lane to position yourself in, though its condition and width varies. Nevertheless it does enable you to keep somewhat separate from the traffic.

As you come closer to central Hobart you will notice the start of a rough footpath on the left. Ride on it as far as it goes, as by now the volume of traffic is increasing. A little further on again—only about 2 km from the city center—as the road ascends and curves to the right there is a footpath/cyclepath on the left. It is in pretty poor condition, but it is advisable that you take it for safety's sake.

At the top of the hill you curve left and run down into Hobart and journey's end.

Hobart

Hobart (pop. 128,603) is a gracious, relaxing little city of fine colonial buildings and lovely ocean views. It occupies a magnificent setting situated on both sides of the Derwent River, under the lofty peak of Mt. Wellington. Founded in 1804 by Colonel David Collins, it is Australia's second-oldest city after Sydney.

There are more than ninety buildings that have a National Trust classification (i.e., they are of considerable historical significance). Salamanca Place, for example, has a lovely terrace of Georgian warehouses dating back to the 1830s, which are now shops and cafes. On Saturdays a lively market is held there. Battery Point, close to Salamanca Place, also has some interesting period architecture and something of a village atmosphere, with narrow streets, restaurants, galleries, and antique shops. Hobart has a good selection of restaurants, and the local seafood is of excellent quality. In recent years Tasmania has acquired a reputation for fine produce, especially seafood, cheese, and berries.

Because it is a relatively small city, Hobart is great just to stroll around at your leisure. There are lots of organized trips and tours that you can take if that's what you enjoy, and there are some you can organize yourself; for example, for a small charge you can tour Cadbury's chocolate factory or the Cascade brewery, the oldest working brewery in Australia.

Bibliography

Travel and Adventure

Australia: A Travel Survival Kit. Hawthorn: Lonely Planet, 1995.

Outback Australia. Hawthorn: Lonely Planet, 1994.

Fielding's Australia. Rodondo Beach, CA: Fielding Travel Guides, 1993.

McEnally, L and J. McEnally. *The Ultimate Book of Camping and Bushwalking.* Sydney: Bay Books, 1994.

Hawthorne S. and R. Klein(eds). *Australia for Women: Travel & Culture* Melbourne: Spinifex Press, 1994.

Cronin L. *Key Guide to Australia's National Parks.* Melbourne: Reed Books, 1995.

Hemmings, L. *Bicycle Touring in Australia.* East Roseville (Australia): Simon & Schuster; Seattle (U.S.A.): The Moutaineers, 1991.

History

Blainey, G. *A Shorter History of Australia.* Melbourne: Mandarin, 1995.

Fitzpatrick, J. *The Bicycle and the Bush.* Melbourne: Oxford University Press, 1980.

Flannery, T. *The Future Eaters: An Ecological History of the Australian Lands and People.* Victoria: Reed Books, 1995.

Aboriginal People and Culture

Broome, R. *Aboriginal Australians.* London: Allen & Unwin, 1994.

Morgan, S. *My Place.* Fremantle: Arts Centre Press, 1989.

Literature

Winton, T. *An Open Swimmer.* Ringwood: Penguin Australia, 1987.

Winton, T. *The Riders.* Sydney: Pan, 1995.

Pictorial

Smolan, R . and A. Park (eds). *A Day in the Life of Australia.* San Francisco: Harper-Collins, 1981.

Facts and Figures

Nicholson, M. *The Little Aussie Fact Book.* Ringwood: Penguin Australia, 1995.

Index

Other Titles Available from Bicycle Books

Title	Author	US Price
All Terrain Biking	Jim Zarka	$7.95
The Backroads of Holland	Helen Colijn	$12.95
The Bicycle Commuting Book	Rob van der Plas	$7.95
The Bicycle Fitness Book	Rob van der Plas	$7.95
The Bicycle Repair Book	Rob van der Plas	$9.95
Bicycle Repair Step by Step (color)*	Rob van der Plas	$14.95
Bicycle Technology	Rob van der Plas	$16.95
Bicycle Touring International	Kameel Nasr	$18.95
The Bicycle Touring Manual	Rob van der Plas	$16.95
Bicycling Fuel	Richard Rafoth	$9.95
Cycling Australia	Ian Duckworth	$14.95
Cycling Canada	John Smith	$12.95
Cycling Europe	Nadine Slavinski	$12.95
Cycling Great Britain	Hughes & Cleary	$14.95
Cycling Kenya	Kathleen Bennett	$12.95
Cycling the Mediterranean	Kameel Nasr	$14.95
Cycling the San Francisco Bay Area	Carol O'Hare	$12.95
Cycling the U.S. Parks	Jim Clark	$12.95
Cycling in Cyberspace	Kienholz & Pawlak	$14.95
A Guide to Cycling Injuries*	Domhnall MacAulley	$12.95
In High Gear (hardcover)	Samuel Abt	$21.95
The High Performance Heart	Maffetone & Mantell	$10.95
The Mountain Bike Book	Rob van der Plas	$10.95
Mountain Bike Maintenance (color)	Rob van der Plas	$10.95
Mountain Bikes: Maint. & Repair*	Stevenson & Richards	$22.50
Mountain Biking the National Parks	Jim Clark	$12.95
Roadside Bicycle Repair (color)	Rob van der Plas	$7.95
Tour of the Forest Bike Race (color)	H.E. Thomson	$9.95
Cycle History – 4th Intern. Conference Proceedings (hardcover)		$30.00
Cycle History – 5th Intern. Conference Proceedings (hardcover)		$45.00

Buy our books at your local book store or bike shop.

If you have difficulty obtaining our books elsewhere, we will be pleased to supply them by mail, but we must add $2.50 postage and handling, or $3.50 for priority mail (and California sales tax if mailed to a California address). Prepayment by check or credit card must be included.

Bicycle Books, Inc.
1282 - 7th Avenue
San Francisco, CA 94122, U.S.A.
Tel.   (415) 665-8214
FAX (415) 753-8572

In Britain: Bicycle Books
463 Ashley Road
Poole, Dorset BH14 0AX
Tel.   (01202) 71 53 49
FAX (01202) 73 61 91

---

* Books marked thus not available from Bicycle Books in the U.K.